Scripture-based Solutions to
HANDLING
STRESS

Pat King

LIGUORI
PUBLICATIONS

One Liguori Drive
Liguori, Missouri 63057-9999
(314) 464-2500

Imprimi Potest:
James Shea, C.SS.R.
Provincial, St. Louis Province
The Redemptorists

Imprimatur:
Monsignor Maurice F. Byrne
Vice Chancellor, Archdiocese of St. Louis

ISBN 0-89243-332-9
Library of Congress Catalog Card Number: 90-62653

Copyright © 1990, Liguori Publications
Printed in U.S.A.

Scripture selections are taken from the NEW AMERICAN BIBLE WITH REVISED NEW TESTAMENT, copyright © 1986, by the Confraternity of Christian Doctrine, Washington, DC 20017, and are used by permission of copyright owner. All rights reserved.

"Social Readjustment Rating Scale" is reprinted from *The Journal of Psychosomatic Research,* 11:213-218, Thomas H. Holmes, Professor of Psychiatry and Behavioral Sciences, copyright © 1967, Pergamon Press PLC.

Cover Design: Chris Sharp

Contents

How to Use This Book 4

"I've Been There Too" — The Author's Story 6

Part One: Defining the Problem 10
   Lesson *1*: Our Bodies Under Stress 11
   Lesson *2*: The Stress of Not Being Appreciated 21
   Lesson *3*: Difficult Transitions 34
   Lesson *4*: Continuing Stress 47

Part Two: Finding Solutions 63
   Lesson *5*: Setting Priorities 64
   Lesson *6*: The Eight-Part Plan for Taking Care
               of Your Body 71
   Lesson *7*: Energy Levels 85
   Lesson *8*: The Importance of Saying No 93
   Lesson *9*: Friends, the Ultimate Support System 104
   Lesson 10: Making Peace Through Reconciliation 114
   Lesson 11: Letting Go of the Past
               Through Forgiveness 121
   Lesson 12: The Secret of Energy 129
   Continuing On: Helps for Further Progress 137
   The I-Gain-Control-of-My-Life Chart 140

How to Use This Book

Today most of us travel under an incredible amount of stress. As we go into the twenty-first century, the loads we carry are probably greater than stress loads have been at any other time in history. We come from all walks of life to experience multiple pressures that at one time existed for only a few — those who were "at the top."

Now at every turn, people confess that they can't go on. They are so tired, so worn down, so *stressed.* It's because our present culture puts such a burden of accomplishment on us. So many of our childhoods have conditioned us to feel we must live up to the expectations of others. So many of us drive ourselves to be successful. So few of us accept ourselves unconditionally.

Many of us are Christians who, on top of all the other urgencies, feel we must do our part to spread the gospel. We must teach the Good News, battle pornography, serve the poor, and so on. It's called the "Martha Complex," referring to the overly busy Martha who urged Jesus to get her sister to help her. (See Luke 10:38-42.) The Martha Complex is functioning when we serve God and others in order to prove our own worth.

All this stress leads to what psychologist Herbert Freudenberger calls burnout — a depletion of energy and a feeling of being overwhelmed by others' problems. We victims of burnout suffer such physical and emotional exhaustion that we want people to just go away and leave us alone. Yet the exact opposite often occurs. There's always something more to do, another crisis to face, another accomplishment to take on, another person who claims our energy, until the day comes when there are no more choices to be made. Our energy is gone, gobbled up by a hungry horde of stressful situations.

What we need to understand is that there are ways to quit feeding ourselves to life's demands. This workbook draws on scriptural advice, professional research, and the well of my own experience with burnout. I've written this workbook to help you find a way out of exhaustion and into personal restoration.

As we start our journey, some of the exercises may seem like too much to do. If that's the case, walk where you are comfortable. But do use some of each lesson every week for twelve weeks, and follow the advice. Energy will begin to return as the chapters go by and you learn to deal with the energy-depleting stresses of your life.

These lessons can be done with a spouse, friend, or small group of friends, if you'd like. If you choose to do things that way, each person should do the lesson alone at home and then come together with the other person(s) later in the week to discuss the Scripture passages and share written responses. Journal entries are usually not shared. Whichever way you go, stick with the lessons, and this workbook will make a difference in your life.

"I've Been There Too"
The Author's Story

One early autumn morning many years ago, I realized that something was wrong with my body. I was on a trail, alone, halfway up a mountain. The beautiful morning was so beckoning I'd decided to climb the mountain that rose behind the grounds at a retreat house I was visiting. Now I wished I hadn't gone alone. I felt so, well…so *strange*. The climb was steep, yes, but that didn't account for the dizzy, floating feeling in my head or the unfamiliar weakness in my legs. A silly thought crossed my mind. *Wouldn't it be funny if the women down at the retreat went in for their morning session and I, the retreat speaker, wasn't there?* I wondered how long it would take them to find my body up there on the mountain.

Even with these kinds of thoughts, I pushed on a little further. I had planned to hike to the mountaintop and hated to fall short of my own goal. But the strange feeling persisted to the point where I was actually alarmed. Finally, I turned around and started back down the mountainside. Just as I arrived at the base, the retreat coordinator met me. "Can we get a cup of tea and talk?" she asked. I felt like I needed to lie down or go eat something…*anything* but talk to another person. Instead I agreed, and we took our tea to a lakeside bench. I couldn't concentrate on the woman's words. She wanted my opinion on something, but I couldn't comprehend what.

Finally, breakfast was announced. I was hungry beyond words. After my talk the night before, a woman had wanted to "share her story" with me. In listening, I'd missed the evening snack. Breakfast was cinnamon rolls and oatmeal. I'm allergic to bread, so all I ate was a small dish of oatmeal. Someone offered to ask the cook to fix me an egg. I shook my head: I didn't want to be a bother. Besides, the warm dish of oatmeal had made me feel better.

Three hours later I still hadn't given my talk. There were singing, announcements, and testimonies. I tried to sing "What a Friend We Have in Jesus," but it took too much energy. I put my head on the back of the chair in front of me and waited.

All I wanted to do was stretch out on a nearby table and go to sleep. At last they called on me, but I had only spoken for a short while when I began to realize that the talk was taking more energy than I had left in my body to give. I quit speaking and told the women I thought I was going to faint. What actually happened was more like stopping in suspended animation rather than fainting. Following that exhausting experience, I did little else until spring.

The problem, however, did not begin at the retreat. It had started years before and grown in proportion as, one by one, our ten children entered their teen years. In the beginning the crises were small and came one at a time. My husband, Bill, and I were still young, and we had lots of energy to handle them. Then the troubles doubled and tripled as a covey of children with differing personalities struggled through their own journeys toward independence and maturity.

Bill and I felt our strength wavering as problems developed at every level — from dyslexia in the youngest, to substance abuse in the middle, to marriage problems for the oldest. It seemed like every week brought us something to face — episodes we somehow thought we'd never have to go through. Most stressful of all was the fact that we were holding ourselves responsible for the problems. "If only we'd been stricter," we'd say some days. Other days we'd lament, "If only we'd been more lenient." So many conversations started with the words, "Maybe if we'd done it differently...."

Then one day came the worst crisis of all. Paul, our sixth child, died in an accident. I remember how brave we were at the time. The bravery came partly from our trust in God and partly from the grieving gift of denial. When the denial wore off, we again blamed ourselves. We thought things like *Maybe if we'd trusted God more when the accident happened, our faith would have caused God to spare him....Maybe if we hadn't delighted in Paul's achievements so much....Maybe if we'd been more tolerant of his junky old cars blocking the driveway....* There was only one area where we didn't rile ourselves. We didn't have to say, "If only we'd loved him more." We knew we'd loved this happy-go-lucky son with all our hearts.

We knew nothing about stress or the toll it takes on our bodies. We knew nothing of the information contained in this workbook. I think we believed that if we were good enough Christians, the hurt would somehow go away. We didn't talk about it, pray with anyone else about it, or consider that our bodies were as broken as our emotions. The only thing we knew how to do was ignore the pain and hope it would go away.

Eighteen months after Paul's death, Bill entered the hospital for open-heart surgery. Later, we read that major surgery often happens within eighteen months of the death of a beloved person. There in the hospital Bill looked so much like Paul, and like Paul, he did not respond as he should. His roommate went home and, despite a host of prayers, Bill stayed on. I began to feel like my head was disengaged from my body. Just to drive the twenty-five miles each day to the hospital seemed like a physical impossibility.

Our daughter was getting married in four weeks, and all the planning went on in an endless gray blur. Friends who came to see Bill asked how I was doing. I told them, "I'm just fine." It didn't occur to me that it would be a good idea, or even okay, to admit my weakness and weariness and ask for help.

Then as the days went by, Bill got better and came home. We

had the wedding. Bill began walking two miles a day and finally returned to work. Everybody was fine — except me. Life became more difficult as every day I had less and less energy. At one point I mentioned to Bill that maybe we should go to Hawaii and rest. But he replied that he was fine now. There was nothing wrong with that reply; I had never learned to state my needs in ways that someone could help me meet them. Some days I felt like I could hardly handle all the things I had to do. Still I continued on. And then it was September and the retreat....

What I'm saying to you in this long preamble is, if you are overtired, overburdened, or overextended — if you feel like a failure or as if you are all to blame or that you can't go on, I understand. If life has become such a downward spiral of circumstances that reversing what is happening appears too difficult, there is a way you can find help.

This workbook will help you take charge of your life and defeat the helpless feeling and downward trend. By reading and working with the text and Scripture of the first four lessons, you will come to understand why you feel the way you do. You'll find that your feelings of distress and weariness are normal and that you are not alone.

By reading and working with the text and Scriptures of the next eight lessons, you'll begin to take charge of your life. As you record your progress, you will be able to see the areas where you are gaining control.

The Scriptures will encourage you that God loves and understands you and that you are not alone. Praying and journaling will add depth to your progress by helping you place your trust in God.

So come along with me and we'll work it out together.

Pat King

PART ONE:
Defining
the Problem

Lesson One
Our Bodies Under Stress

Okay, you're ready to begin. Perhaps the baby is in bed for a nap, and you are sitting at the dining-room table. Or perhaps you have come in from a long day at work, and you are stretched out in the big chair in the living room. Maybe you are waiting in your car for a soccer practice or a piano lesson to be over. It doesn't really matter where you are as you do this first lesson. The important thing is that you have begun it. Every Tuesday morning or Thursday evening or whatever is best for you, it's time to get a pencil, Bible, notebook, and this workbook and retreat to your own special spot.

This lesson is your commitment to yourself so that you can get a handle on the stress of your life. But you can't do it alone, and you don't have to, for the Lord is very willing to be your partner. Invite him in now by slowly and reverently praying:

Dear God, today I start a special journey. I invite you and Jesus to come with me. I invite your Holy Spirit to guide me. I look forward to this time together that will help me understand the stress I'm under and that will help me gain control of my life. Thank you for the complex combination of body, will, intellect, emotions, and spirit that is me.

Glory be to the Father, and to the Son, and to the Holy Spirit, as it was in the beginning, is now, and ever shall be, world without end. Amen.

Write here how you think the Lord responds to this prayer.

_____

_____

We'll be using this prayer often throughout the book. If you'd like to say an inclusive language version of the same prayer, you can pray, "Glory be to the Creator, and to the Redeemer, and to the Sanctifier...."

This lesson tells how wonderfully our bodies are made and how they and our emotions may be affected by the crises in our lives. This lesson and the three others that follow it offer no solutions. Their purpose is to put you in touch with the number of stressful demands in your life and your physical and emotional response to those demands.

To begin, picture yourself carrying a portable television up and down a flight of stairs twenty times. By nighttime, or surely by the next morning, your body would feel the aches and pains of such intense exercise. You might even say, "I'm not carrying that television up those stairs one more time!"

In the same way, the multitudes of stress-causing crises that you endure also affect your body. Even though the aches and pains of too much stress are hard to define at first, they are there. Unless you have a physical disability, God has made your body capable of picking up a portable television and taking it up and down stairs. The problem comes when the situations in your life cause stress after stress after stress. Such problems get to be too much to carry around, but unlike refusing to carry a television, you are probably not so easily able to call a halt to the buildup of stress within your body.

To begin understanding, let's look at the way your body is made.

Read Deuteronomy 4:32. What word describes your creation by God?_____

Read Psalm 139:13, 14. How does the psalmist describe the creation of your body? It is _____ and _____ made.

Read Acts 17:28. Fill in the missing words of the following sentence: It is in God that we _____ and _____ and have _____   _____.

What do these passages say to you about your body?

_____

_____

Truly the composition of our bodies is wonderful. One of the most amazing aspects of our physical being is the way God created us to deal with crises.

Imagine that you are being followed on a dark street by a man with a mask over his face. Or imagine that you have to rush a child to the hospital. Or imagine that you are sitting peacefully by a pool when a man yells, "Help, I'm drowning!" In all these cases your adrenal glands would be superbly equipped to handle such crises. They would send a flood of adrenaline and noradrenaline through your body to give you extraordinary ability to either flee the danger or fight it. In seconds this action from your adrenal glands would

• constrict the arteries and make the heart beat faster, thus rushing blood to the muscles and brain.

- draw the blood back from the skin.
- raise the white blood cell count (in case of infection).
- increase the red blood cell count (for a greater supply of fuel).
- stimulate the muscles and liver to release sugar into the blood.
- cause the pancreas to pour insulin into the blood.
- stop the digestive tract from functioning in order to save energy.

All this happens in a matter of seconds. This action gives you incredible strength to flee that would-be mugger, rush the child to the hospital, or rescue the drowning man. Dr. Hans Selye, the "granddaddy" of stress research, calls this occurrence the "fight or flight response." Your body has been made to either flee or throw itself into battle when it is confronted with a crisis.

When the crisis is over, if you understand this wonderful working of your body, you can thank God for the surge of adrenaline that was there at the exact instant you needed it.

Now let's assume that you haven't met up with a mugger or a child's emergency or a drowning man or any such physical situation. But you probably have had to deal with any combination of the following situations:

- an angry coworker,
- a careless driver,
- a helpless older person,
- an indifferent caseworker,
- a hostile teenager,
- an absentee spouse,
- a leaking roof,
- a lost paycheck,
- a letter saying you've inherited a fortune (good things cause stress in your body too).

In all these crises, adrenaline would flood your body just as it would if you faced a physical emergency. But in these examples there's no reason to flee for your life. There's nothing to physically fight, and there's no one to rescue from physical danger. Yet your endocrine system, heart, muscles, liver, pancreas, and digestive system are all geared for battle. Without a physical outlet, it takes seventy-two hours for your body to return to normal.

Unfortunately, for many of us there is rarely a seventy-two-hour wait between crises. They come one on top of the other so that our bodies don't fully recuperate from one episode before the next episode hits. This continuing adrenal arousal batters our bodies day after day after day.

Ponder: What does the above explanation help you understand about the way your body has been feeling? Even though the preceding facts give an extremely simplified view of the complex interaction within your body, how do they increase your understanding of the Scriptures that tell how wonderfully you are made?

What Exactly Is Stress?

Stress has been defined by Dr. Hans Selye as the nonspecific response of the body to any demand made on it. This means that all the demands made on us will cause a response in our bodies. Both crises and not-so-urgent demands placed on us will eventually elicit a body response.

The wheel illustrated on the next page will help you better visualize and comprehend the demands of your life situation. Write your name in the center. On the spokes, write the names of each person who your life touches daily or weekly. Add extra spokes if needed. Add a double spoke for a difficult boss, any child under two, any teenager, or a dependent or elderly person. Add four spokes for an abusive spouse. Add a longer spoke for each member of your extended family (for example, parents, grandparents, grandchildren, ex-spouse, stepchildren) who in any way comes into your life. Finally, don't forget to include coworkers, neighbors, grown children, in-laws, salespeople, teachers, caseworkers, or anyone else who is an important part of your life on a daily or weekly basis.

The Stress Wheel

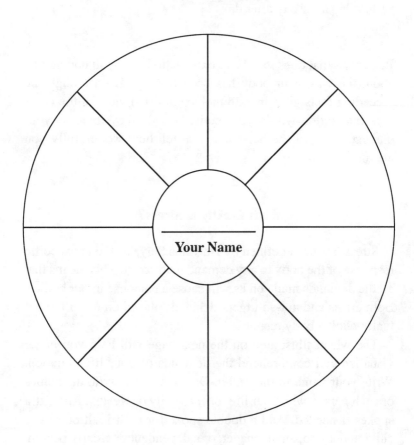

Your Name

Ponder: How many spokes (demands) do you have to deal with in a week (not counting the crises)? _____ Does your personalized wheel give you a clearer idea of how much stress you are under?

If your physical body is feeling this stressed, what happens to you emotionally? Check and see if any of the situations described below apply to you.

- Your brain seems mushy; you can't concentrate.
- You forget what you were saying and where you put things.
- Experiences that never used to confuse you, such as going grocery shopping, now bewilder you.
- You cry easily or feel like crying more often than you ever have before.
- Something that wouldn't have bothered you last year, such as the pastor being too busy to talk, hurts your feelings now.
- You're irritable.
- You feel like a failure.
- Prayer, which was once easier, is now difficult.

Write here similar areas where you are not as in control as you used to be.

_____

_____

_____

If you push yourself long enough, as I did, you reach the stage of burnout. Burnout is characterized by loss of enthusiasm, energy, idealism, perspective, and purpose. It is a state of mental, physical, and spiritual exhaustion brought on by continued stress.

Below are five stages of a person in the process of getting burned out. It's possible that you may find yourself at any stage:

1. *Physiological stage:* Characterized by feelings of fatigue and strain. Person may suffer from physical ailments.

2. *Social stage:* Characterized by feelings of irritability. Person becomes difficult to deal with and starts to avoid people.

3. *Intellectual stage:* Person gives up trying to reason or think things through.

4. *Psycho-emotional stage:* Person feels like he or she is always trying to meet other people's needs. There is a strong desire to be alone. Dependence on alcohol or drugs (if it occurs) is most likely to begin at this stage.

5. *Introspective stage:* Person is less and less willing to help others and becomes selfish.

All this occurs while a person is trying to meet the demands and pressures of life. The human body was not made to live under constant stress. Something gives if it is forced to endure such stress. God knows your pressure and understands your body and your situation far better than you do. The good news is that there is a way out for you.

Read Genesis 28:15. God promises not to _____ you.

Read Psalm 121:5. God is your _____ .

Read Psalm 115:12. The Lord _____ you and _____ _____ you.

Read Luke 12:7. God even knows the _____ on your head.

Read 1 Peter 5:7. God _____ for you.

Read 2 Timothy 1:12. God is able to _____ you.

Journaling

For many people, writing a journal is a great stress reliever. A journal is between yourself and God. Penmanship, punctuation, grammar, and spelling don't matter. No one has to see your journal but you. For these lessons the journal experience will usually be to ask God a question in writing or tell God something and then record what you think God's response would be.

This week's journal experience is to tell God how you secretly feel about the way your life is going right now. Record how you think God would respond.

Wrap Up

This is enough for today. In closing, ask yourself: *Which of the above Scriptures makes me feel less vulnerable and less alone? Which one speaks to me most clearly about God's understanding of my stressful situation?*

_____

_____

Gaining control: On page 140 fill in the *I-Gain-Control-of-My-Life Chart* for lesson one.

Continue during the week: This week pay special attention to what is going on in your body. After you have been scared or angry or in some other way upset, write here what changes you discerned in your physical body (heart beating faster, dizziness, edginess, fidgeting, sweating, cold hands, and so on).

_____

_____

_____

Just for fun: Draw a picture of the way you look when you are upset. Use colored pens or pencils. Share your picture with someone.

Memorize:
    Truly you have formed my inmost being;
        you knit me in my mother's womb.
    I give you thanks that I am fearfully, wonderfully made;
        wonderful are your works.
    My soul also you knew full well.

                    (Psalm 139:13, 14)

Closing prayer:
Dear God, thank you for caring about every aspect of my body and my life. Help me find your solutions to my needs.

Glory be to the Father, and to the Son, and to the Holy Spirit, as it was in the beginning, is now, and ever shall be, world without end. Amen.

Lesson Two
The Stress of Not Being Appreciated

Beginning prayer:
Dear God, help me appreciate the beautiful world that you have created and given to me.

Glory be to the Father, and to the Son, and to the Holy Spirit, as it was in the beginning, is now, and ever shall be, world without end. Amen.

The Lesson: Dealing With Your Needs for Appreciation

Nonreciprocity is one of the major, but little considered, reasons our bodies come to feel overloaded. We can feel like we're taken for granted, whether we are young or old, working outside or inside the home, poor or well-off, and so on. Nonreciprocity is an equal-opportunity employer. If we mingle for long with other people, many of us will experience the building stress that comes from day-by-day living with people who take our contributions for granted.

Bodily stress often builds in such thin layers that we don't even realize there's a building project going on inside us. It's like the way that one single sheet of newspaper does not make the Sunday edition. Yet sheet by sheet the pile of papers does start to stack up. We've all experienced how a pile of newspapers can grow until it falls over and scatters. At that point we know the papers need to be cleared out. *How did there get to be such a mess here?* you may ask yourself in this situation. The answer is *Little by little it adds up.* One of the thin layers of stress that stacks up so slowly that we don't notice it is the stress of not being appreciated.

Al has gone twice a week for fifteen years to care for his aging grandmother. The old lady pouts, complains, and refuses to say thank you.

Patrice gave up her Christmas money to buy her daughter a skirt. Instead of thanks, her daughter yelled, "I hate this skirt!"

Colin has given up many lunch hours to work on reports and speeches for a boss who never bothers to say she appreciates Colin's effort.

Rhonda works all day at her job as a retail salesperson and then comes home to cook, shop, launder, and clean for a nonappreciative household that complains when dinner isn't ready.

Raul has given help and money to a friend and has listened to his woes. Yet this "friend" invites others to go out to a sporting event, but not Raul.

Zita drives sixty miles each day to take care of her grandchildren while her daughter works. Zita's poor health means that some days she struggles to get out of bed. Yet she makes herself go. Her daughter is so preoccupied with the difficulties of her own life that she never thinks to listen to her mother's problems or to give any thanks.

These people are the givers of this world. Their pasts have shaped them into people who want to help others. Still, they all admit that giving can drain them. Each would like the recipients of their giving to give heartfelt thanks. Not only would appreciation be welcome, but it would also help to ease the load.

The reason we often don't see the stress of not being appreciated is that most of us don't want to admit that we feel burdened by others' demands or expectations. It sounds so petty. Certainly, a Christian is not supposed to count the cost of giving and giving. Somehow we think it's not supposed to matter that no one appreciates our efforts.

Read Luke 17:11-18 to see how Jesus felt when others did not appreciate him. What had Jesus done for the ten men?

_____

_____

_____

What did he expect in return?

_____

_____

_____

Yes, even Jesus was disappointed in the lack of appreciation from the men whose lives had been so drastically changed by his healing power. Why do you think it matters to us when people don't seem to appreciate our efforts on their behalf?

_____

_____

_____

Read Genesis 40. Write why you think Pharaoh's winetaster ("cupbearer" in some Bibles) forgot all about Joseph.

_____

_____

_____

How do you think Joseph felt in prison when he realized he'd been forgotten by the wine servant?

_____

_____

_____

_____

Read Judges 8:22. What did Gideon do for the people of Israel?

_____

_____

Read Judges 8:35. How did the people treat Gideon's family?

_____

_____

Read 1 Samuel 25:4-11. What does David ask of Nabal?

_____

_____

What is Nabal's reply?

_____

_____

How do you think David felt when Nabal refused to help him after David had helped guard his sheep?

_____

_____

Read Ecclesiastes 9:14-15. What had the wise man done?

_____

_____

_____

_____

Who appreciated it? _____

Pretend you are the wise man in this passage. How do you think you'd feel?

_____

_____

Yes, failing to appreciate others, it seems, is normal to the human condition.

Ponder: When have you ever been ungrateful?

I remember a Christmas day with our ten children as well as the older ones' spouses and the little grandchildren. No one had really helped with dinner. No one cleaned up for more than five minutes immediately after the meal, and by the time I got out of the kitchen, everyone was ready to leave. They said, "Good-bye, Mom. Merry Christmas!" I remember how I felt watching them go. I resentfully said to myself, _All that work, and I didn't even get to talk to anyone!_ I felt used and bone-weary. I told myself, _A true Christian would have been glad to be a willing servant to her family._ That made me feel like a failure. Now, a little older and wiser than I was then, I have learned to _ask_ for help from those around me. I know that working until I'm exhausted distorts my thinking. Feeling used is never a pleasant experience, no matter how Christian I am.

Appreciation Checklist

List below things you do for your parish or community.

_____

_____

_____

_____

_____

Put an **X** by those things that people let you know they appreciate. How do you feel about the approval you receive from these activities?

_____

_____

_____

If you have a paid or volunteer job, list here the extra help you give to other people.

_____

_____

_____

_____

_____

On the previous page put an **X** beside those extras that the people you work with let you know they appreciate.

List here the things you do for family or friends.

_____

_____

_____

_____

Put an **X** beside the things your family or friends show appreciation for. How do you feel about their response to all that you do for them?

_____

_____

_____

Now that you've done this exercise, who can you see appreciates you most?

_____

_____

Who appreciates you least?

_____

_____

In what part of your life do you feel least appreciated?

_____

_____

Where is the stress of unappreciation tending to add up and get out of hand in your life?

_____

_____

_____

Read Isaiah 43:1-24. What has God promised his people?

"When you pass through the water _____

_____."

"In the rivers _____."

"When you walk through fire _____

_____."

What does God assure us of in verse 5 of this reading from Isaiah?

_____

_____

_____

In verse 7?_____

In verse 11? _____

In verse 12?_____

In verse 15? _____

In verse 16? _____

In verse 17? _____

In verse 24? _____

Overall, what does this passage from Isaiah tell you about the way God feels about being unappreciated?

_____

_____

_____

Write out what this tells you about how God understands the way you feel about being unappreciated.

_____

_____

_____

There are ways we can insist on change in this area of not being appreciated, and we will get to those in part two of this workbook, which is about solutions. But there are some situations that nobody and nothing can change. You are a giver because that is the way you operate. The people who take what you give and fail to appreciate it will probably keep on taking you for granted because unappreciation is so normal. For now, here are a couple of things you can do.

Read Ezekiel 16:8-63. The words in this passage are a strong passionate speech God gave through the prophet Ezekiel. In the speech God is addressing the depths of Israel's failure. Can you put into one word the way God is going to treat these people despite what they have done to him? _____

Go back to your Appreciation Checklist and find a person who simply does not appreciate what you do for him or her. Think of a kindly act you can do for this person, something that will bless him or her, even if you know it's not going to be appreciated. Write it down at the top of the next page.

_____

_____

Will you mind doing it? _____

Knowing that we won't always be appreciated may be the best antidote for the stress of unappreciation.

Wrap Up

Gaining control: On page 140 fill in the *I-Gain-Control-of-My-Life Chart* for lesson two.

Continue during the week: List here the good things others do for you in your parish and/or community.

_____

_____

_____

_____

_____

At work _____

_____

_____

_____

_____

Within your circle of family and friends

_____

_____

_____

_____

_____

What are some of the good things God does for you?

_____

_____

_____

_____

_____

Choose one item in each of the four lists you've just made and decide how you will show your appreciation. Often a word of gratitude is all that is needed.

Just for fun: Give yourself an appreciation gift.

Journal experience: Your journal is also a good place to record your insights, special Scriptures, or parts of sermons you want to hang on to. You can even include the surprisingly wise words a child said or that terrible scene between you and your teenager. Remember, your journal is a place of complete honesty between you and God. It will help you get in touch with workings of the Holy Spirit in your life, as well as help you know yourself better. This week ask the Holy Spirit to show you where you can grow in appreciation of God. Record how the Holy Spirit answers.

Memorize: "Jesus said in reply, 'Ten were cleansed, were they not? Where are the other nine?' " (Luke 17:17).

Weekly log exercise: For this week and the next two weeks' lessons, this weekly log exercise will help you get a better idea of just what it is that is causing stress in your life.

For each day during the coming week, write down the times when you feel like you are not being appreciated for what you do or who you are. Then after each incident, give it a "stress rating" on a scale of one to ten (with ten being the highest amount of stress). For example: *Because nobody else does it, I cleaned up the lunchroom at work, even though it's not really my job.* Stress rating: 8.

Day 1 _____

_____

_____ Stress rating: _____

Day 2 _____

_____

_____ Stress rating: _____

Day 3 _____

_____

_____ Stress rating: _____

Day 4 _____

_____

_____ Stress rating: _____

Day 5 _____

_____

_____ Stress rating: _____

Day 6 _____

_____

_____ Stress rating: _____

Day 7 _____

_____

_____ Stress rating: _____

Closing prayer:

Dear God, thank you for your loving care and for promising to never ever leave me.

Glory be to the Father, and to the Son, and to the Holy Spirit, as it was in the beginning, is now, and ever shall be, world without end. Amen.

Lesson Three
Difficult Transitions

Beginning prayer:
Dear God, thank you for my life and all its circumstances.
Glory be to the Father, and to the Son, and to the Holy Spirit, as it was in the beginning, is now, and ever shall be, world wihout end. Amen.

The Lesson: Learning to Deal With Change

Change is never easy, and that makes it stressful. In the last lesson we talked about how not being appreciated can cause stress to build gradually in our lives the same way that thin layers of newspapers can build up. In this lesson we will see that there are transitions in our lives that cause stress to build in ways that are more like stacking bricks than newspapers. It doesn't take many of these bricks to cause heaviness in our lives.

The most difficult transition, according to the stress charts, is the death of a spouse. Are you recently widowed? If so, you may have lived with your spouse for thirty or more years. You had no doubt tuned your life to your spouse's idiosyncrasies. All sorts of mundane things like mealtimes, roles, and everyday conversations are all thrown out of kilter when a spouse dies. Everything is changed. Money can become a critical issue. Sex can become an unspoken issue. The future can become a fearful issue.

If you are an older person, you may find yourself cooking and eating alone. Alone you figure the income tax and insurance. Alone you go to a son's or daughter's birthday dinner. For a long time after a spouse's death, every day brings something new to be faced differently than it was before.

If you are young when a spouse dies, you suffer the above pains plus you probably face the enormous pressure of rearing children alone. Social contacts dwindle, as people seem to invite only couples. Weariness sets in when there is no one to share the responsibility with and no warm body to soothe away the loneliness and problems of everyday life.

The next most stressful transition is divorce. Take all of the troubles mentioned above and add rejection, guilt, and legal hassles over money, children, and possessions. Add to that the disapproval of family, the suspicions of friends, and a sense of failure and loss. Add the pain of seeing your ex-spouse's new companion. Add the lack of support from the Church and community. Divorce, even when it means living alone, is usually far better than living as a couple in terrible conflict. Yes, divorce brings great stress to the inner workings of your body and emotions if you are faced with such a situation. If you are a single parent, you're faced with the life-changing transition of a child or children in your total care. Such a situation can make you feel as though you're living in a state of chronic stress. There's never enough money; the baby-sitting question is never permanently solved; the transportation situation is never hassle-free. Friends (unless they are single parents too) can't identify with your struggles and tend to slip away, leaving you behind in loneliness.

One area of stress that is not charted too high on the stress charts, yet is extremely stressful for many of us, is the loss of a friend. When a relationship with someone we love shuts down, we respond with anguish. It could be that moving has ended our friendship or that time has separated us. Or it could be that we argued, and that special friend has chosen to be distant. Perhaps we severed the relationship because, even though we loved, the friendship was destroying us. Whatever the reason, to lose a friend alters the way it's always been, and the transition is painful. Some friendships can be as addictive to us as alcohol is to an alcoholic. We can find we need the other person to help us withstand life's pressures, to assure us we have value, to make up for childhood hurts. When that person is gone, we go through a painful withdrawal that no one on earth can make up for.

Perhaps your difficult transition is the uncertainty of a new job. Maybe it's the guilt you feel about being fired. Maybe it's the discomfort involved in having a new roommate. Difficult transitions can include the loss of money or unexpectedly inheriting a fortune. A new house, a new neighborhood, a new school, a new city…all are stressful.

Perhaps your difficult transitions are none of the threatening examples mentioned in this lesson, yet you are still experiencing other changes that are taking their toll. One of the big problems that make crises so hard for us is that we are Christians, and as Christians we feel guilty when we don't smile through the difficulties. I believe that many of us are far too hard on ourselves. We keep listening to that never-satisfied person living way down inside us that tells us we must do better than we're doing. It tells us, "You mustn't feel that way! You must get a grip on yourself." If we succeed at getting that inner person silenced, our friends and family can heap on the guilt, saying things like "What's the matter? Why aren't you over it? Why can't you handle this?" Between our own expectations and our family's and friends' comments, it's easy to stay discouraged. Instead of letting all these unappreciative voices smother our inner spirits, we need to be merciful to ourselves.

Why Transitions Are Difficult

One of the reasons transitions are so inescapably difficult is because our lives set themselves in rhythms that are comfortable. Rhythm in itself is comforting. We depend on spring to follow winter, Saturday to follow Friday, and daylight to follow darkness. We rely on these predictable rhythms to the point that we would feel quite disoriented if a season or a day or a sunrise was obliterated from our lives. We feel more secure when the same patterns occur over and over. These patterns could be healthy or unhealthy. A typical day's healthy rhythm would be getting up at a certain time, doing certain things before breakfast, eating breakfast, going to work or school, the cycle of typical things you do at work or school, stopping at a store on the way home, eating dinner, watching television. Some unhealthy patterns in people's lives include overeating, throwing temper tantrums, staying away from home, and excessive drinking. Your day could be spent taking care of children or taking care of tax accounting. Maybe your day-after-day rhythm also means giving care to a sick or elderly person. Maybe your orchestrated rhythm is a combination of all the above, with the added staccato of teenagers. Whatever it is, let's take a look at it.

The Rhythms of Your Life

Use the following exercise to help you get a better idea of what the predictable rhythms in your life are. If you work during an evening or night shift, adjust your answers accordingly.

I wake up at _____.

Before breakfast I do the following things:

_____

_____

_____

_____

I usually eat _____ for breakfast.

After I eat I do the following things:

_____

_____

_____

_____

My morning is usually filled with the following types of activities:

_____

_____

_____

_____

In the afternoon I usually do these things:

_____

_____

_____

_____

I usually start thinking about dinner at this time: _____.

In the evening I do this:

_____

_____

_____

_____

What Happens When the Rhythm Changes?

If something comes along and changes your daily rhythm, you don't feel its effect right away. A change in your daily rhythm can happen if friends come to stay for a few days, if the car needs major repairs, if you take responsibility for a strong-willed child for a week. During the first seventy-two hours of any of these transitions (or breaks in rhythm), you usually can adapt pretty well. But by the fourth day your body begins sending messages that it doesn't like this new regimen. You begin to want your friends to leave, even though you've enjoyed them; taking the bus or getting lifts because your car is out of commission becomes a time-consuming headache; the strong-willed child becomes intolerable.

Write here the similar *mild* changes you have endured lately.

_____

_____

_____

_____

_____

_____

As uncomfortable as these are, you can adapt to them if you know they are God's will for you. If your friends moved in for a year, you would begin to develop a new rhythm that would include them being there, and they would cease to be a burden. (This is presuming that their presence does not create any other problems — a rather large presumption.) If your friends are pleasant, it would take four to eight weeks for the new rhythm to develop. If they are unpleasant but you are willing to lay down your life because you feel their being there is God's will, it will take eight to sixteen weeks to adjust. If they are unpleasant and you are not convinced this is what God is asking of you, then your whole body will fight against it until you are so sick that they will have to leave.

The broken-down car is something you can adjust to in four to six weeks. If it just can't be fixed or isn't worth it, you will come to terms with the problem and seek other alternatives. If it can be fixed just as soon as you get the money, you can adapt to that. But if you are waiting for scarce parts coming over on a slow boat from Japan or if your spouse should waste the repair money or there is some other annoying circumstance that keeps the car from getting fixed, it will be difficult to adapt to the new rhythm. Because you keep expecting the car to be fixed, you never quite adjust to the new pattern. This state of nagging uncertainty will eventually affect your physical body if it goes on long enough.

A strong-willed child coming to stay means that the old rhythm is totally destroyed for you and the rest of your household. You've got your own upset rhythm to adjust to as well as everyone else's upset rhythm to cope with. The adjustment, if you are certain God has called you to it, will probably take six to eight weeks. During the adapting time, you will feel mild stress symptoms in your body, but they will go away if you take care of yourself (more on this in chapter four). If you are not convinced having the child stay with you is God's will, then you will probably start feeling stronger stress symptoms in your body in two or three weeks. They will escalate until you are physically unable to watch the child, and someone else has to take over.

All of the above are relatively small transitions. On the next page we will meet some people in the Bible and see the life-changing transitions they faced. See if you can match each character with his or her point of stress/break in rhythm. Take time to look up each Scripture passage, and try to really understand the stress each person must have suffered.

Biblical People Who Suffered
Difficult Transitions

Match the following biblical personalities with the correct transitions they had to deal with.

a. ____ Moses and the Israelites

b. ____ Esther

c. ____ Paul

d. ____ Rebekah and Isaac

e. ____ Jacob

f. ____ Abigail

g. ____ Rizpah and Merob

h. ____ Elizabeth

i. ____ Mary

j. ____ Shecaniah

k. ____ Jonathan and David

l. ____ Hannah

m. ____ Hagar

n. ____ Barnabas and Paul

1. Separation from family (Genesis 21:14-16)

2. Anguish over a child's marriage (Genesis 21:34-35)

3. Loss of a spouse (Genesis 35:16-20)

4. Long-distance move (Exodus 12:31-39)

5. Son or daughter leaving home (1 Samuel 1:24-28)

6. Loss of a friend (1 Samuel 20:35-42)

7. Remarriage (1 Samuel 25:3, 36-42)

8. Death of children (2 Samuel 21:8-10)

9. Divorce (Ezra 10:2-3)

10. Major change in responsibility (Esther 2:17)

11. Pregnancy (Luke 1:24-25)

12. Suffering of a son or daughter (John 19:25)

13. Disagreement in the Church (Acts 15:36-39)

14. Imprisonment (Ephesians 3:1)

Your thoughts: What were your reflections as you considered the stress of these people in biblical times?

_____

_____

_____

_____

_____

_____

_____

_____

Which person's suffering touched you the most? _____

Why? _____

_____

Write down any *major* difficult transitions you are facing.

_____

_____

How long do you feel it will take to adjust to the new rhythm caused by these major events?

_____

_____

Did you allow yourself enough time? If it takes sixteen weeks to adjust to a smaller transition, then it may take far longer to adjust to a larger, life-altering change. If a new transition comes along before you adjust to an earlier one, then the first adjustment can take even longer. Remember to add time for the second transition. If necessary, take into account the time to adjust to a third difficult transition. I've heard highly stressed people say, "I'm so tired these days." Of course they are. They've never rested up from one crisis before the next one hits. Do you want to go back and refigure how long it will take your body to adjust?

In what ways are you going to lower your expectations of your emotions and your body — how you feel physically and emotionally?

_____

_____

_____

_____

_____

_____

From what transition are you going to give yourself more time to adjust?

_____

_____

In times of crisis, it helps to have *one* Bible verse that is yours. It's amazing how one verse can see you through a difficult moment. I remember walking down the street once when my husband, Bill, was back in the hospital. As I walked I was saying my verse over and over: "Now I know that God is with me. Now I know that God is with me...." (See Psalm 56:10.) Finally, the words of that verse hit. At that moment, I knew in my innermost being that God is God and that I could trust him in the setback my husband and I were experiencing.

Bible verses are as varied as people. Here are several that may speak to you.

- Slay me though he might, I will wait for him;
  I will defend my conduct before him (Job 13:15).
- But my trust is in you, O LORD;
  I say, "You are my God" (Psalm 31:15).
- No one who waits for you shall be put to shame (Psalm 25:3).
- For to his angels he has given command about you (Psalm 91:11).
- God indeed is my savior;
  I am confident and unafraid (Isaiah 12:2).
- I know him in whom I have believed and am confident that he is able to guard what has been entrusted to me until that day (2 Timothy 1:12).

Wrap Up

Gaining control: On page 140 fill in the *I-Gain-Control-of-My-Life Chart* for lesson three.

Continue during the week: Keep track of the rhythms of your life. Note what is uncomfortable and what is comforting.

Just for fun: Read a beloved old favorite, even if it's a children's book or story. (My favorite story of all is *The Hiding Place* by Corrie Ten Boom.)

Journal experience: Write out what an ideal day consists of for you. Ask God what your level of maturity might become if every day was this idealistic. Record what you think God's answer might be.

Memorize: Find your own "special verse" in the Bible and commit it to memory.

Weekly log exercise: Write out the transitions in your life that cause you the most difficulty this week. It may be the same one every day, or each day may bring something different. It will be interesting to find out which applies to you.

Day 1 _____

_____

_____

Day 2 _____

_____

_____

Day 3 _____

_____

_____

Day 4 _____

_____

_____

Day 5 _____

_____

_____

Day 6 _____

_____

_____

Day 7 _____

_____

_____

Closing prayer:

Dear Lord, help me to be easy on myself and give myself enough time to adjust to any new rhythms of my life. I am grateful that you aren't in nearly as big a hurry as I am.

Glory be to the Father, and to the Son, and to the Holy Spirit, as it was in the beginning, is now, and ever shall be, world without end. Amen.

Lesson Four
Continuing Stress

Beginning prayer:
Dear God, help me understand myself and what is going on in my life.

Glory be to the Father, and to the Son, and to the Holy Spirit, as it was in the beginning, is now, and ever shall be, world without end. Amen.

The Lesson: Locating and Handling Continuing Stress

In the last two lessons we talked about not being appreciated and difficult transitions. This lesson is about the highly stressful situations that continue on and on in our lives. In this lesson you will be comforted to see that Jesus' life held stress for him too. You'll also find comfort in discovering that you don't always have to be brave in a life of high-stress situations.

Let's look at some lives of continuing stress.

Burt lives with a wife who, because of a stroke, no longer speaks. He has to guess at her thoughts and resigns himself daily to never having a conversation with her. Even though Burt is a physically active person, he finds his life severely curtailed by his wife's limitations.

Sonia discovered that her son has AIDS. He is dying and there are so few she can tell because she doesn't want her friends to condemn him or her. What should she do about him? Go to the city where he lives? Nurse him? Leave her family to fend for themselves? Ask her son to come home? The right solution evades her.

Lana grew up in a poor family. She married a man who works hard but drinks up his paycheck. At age twenty-seven, she's never had a new dress since she's been married. There is no money for adequate groceries, doctors, dentists, or decent housing. Lana is pregnant again and sees no time in the future when her life will be different.

Todd has a boss who doesn't like him. The boss gives others credit for what Todd accomplishes and pays him less than he pays new employees. Todd could complain, but he is certain that if he does, he'll be forced out of his job, and he doesn't know where he could get another one.

Donna has a disapproving husband. Everyone else thinks Al's wonderful. But when Donna and Al are alone, he finds fault constantly. Nothing is done right. She's "too unsociable." She "wastes money." Al says he can't trust her. Al is just like the father Donna wanted to get away from when she married.

Monica wants to marry, but she finds it extremely difficult to find good Christian men to date. She could probably find a man in a singles' bar but not without compromising her beliefs. In a few more years she'll be past childbearing age. She feels angry and cheated.

Mary Lou has two youngsters and a husband who's still in graduate school. She deals daily with a load of housework, car problems, laundry, and meals. Raised as an only child who had little responsibility, Mary Lou would like a shoulder to cry on some days. But as she looks around her, she sees people going through much worse situations who look like they're coping just fine. This makes her feel guilty for even thinking of complaining.

Joe has had a life of medical problems. Just once he would like to go through the week without spending time in a doctor's office or a hospital. He can never participate much in church activities because of his health. He knows people really don't understand.

Elaine lives with a man who will never marry her. Thomas is having an affair with a man he met in a bar. Noel compulsively steals money from his employer. All are Christians. All live with the continuing stress of guilt.

Leroy is in prison. He wishes he could go back and live his whole life over again and not make so many mistakes. His days are spent thinking, *If only I'd had different parents....If only I hadn't gone off with that woman....If only I'd listened to my sister....If only, if only, if only....*

Ed has been going to the same church for forty-five years. He hates what is happening there. Solemn music has been replaced by folk groups and guitars. The pastor talks about homosexuals and abortion, which Ed thinks are not proper subjects for the pulpit. Children are invited to sit around the altar where they distract everyone. Ed's life has always included the Church, but now the Church is a source of continuing discomfort.

Vic is overweight by a hundred pounds. People urge him to diet, but they don't understand that he's tried and tried to lose weight and can't. With a sigh, he says, "Food is my friend, some days my only friend."

Keri, at five feet seven inches, secretly vomits her dinner or purges her body with laxatives because at one hundred five pounds she feels fat. Her husband says he will divorce her if she continues to do this. Threats don't deter her. In Keri's mind, nothing is worse than gaining a pound.

Elaine, Thomas, Lana, and Vic were all victims of childhood sexual abuse. Each feels the stress of lost innocence. Each feels guilty for having "caused" the incest or the fights between parents or the breakup of the family. A sense of shame haunts every day of their lives.

Todd, Donna, Elaine, and Vic were physically and emotionally abused as children. All have married spouses who abuse them. Some have bosses who abuse them too. One of the stresses all these people carry is being "sure" that they are at fault in their abusive situations.

Lana and Noel are adult children of alcoholic parents. They live with the stress of pretending things are fine when they aren't. They don't know what a normal life is, and they hide from any confrontation.

Sonia, Mary Lou, and Keri grew up feeling they had to be perfect or no one could or would love them. They are so hard on themselves that even a hint of failure in their lives is stressful.

A very personal question: What is in your past that makes today's struggle so difficult? Maybe you don't want to write it down because it hurts too much to acknowledge it. If that's the case, try writing it in code: a name, an initial, or a word.

_____

_____

_____

_____

_____

_____

_____

This lesson will not help you eliminate any hurt you've written above, but it will help expose it so that you can fully understand what may be one of the major elements that is causing you to feel stressed out today.

In the previous examples you saw just a few of the continuing stresses that go on in people's lives. Perhaps you saw yourself in one of the examples or in a combination of them. When you consider your continuing stressful situation along with the stress of difficult transitions and not being appreciated, does it surprise you that you feel as weary as you do?

On the other hand, if your situation is not nearly as severe as the examples here, it is important that you not feel ashamed of the stress you feel in your emotions and body. Don't minimize your situation by comparing it to someone else's. You don't have to have a horrible past for stress to have built up in your life. Also remember that stress in itself is neutral — neither good nor bad. It stems from normal body responses. Too much stress affects almost everyone at some time or another.

Let's take a look now at Jesus and the stress he found in his life.

Look up John 14:5-11. Read aloud Jesus' words in the first sentence of verse 9. How do you think Jesus felt when Philip just didn't comprehend who Jesus was? Write out a one-word description. _____

Read Matthew 8:23-27. Jesus was so physically exhausted that he was sleeping through a storm. In one word, how do you think Jesus felt when the disciples awakened him in fear? _____

Read Matthew 16:5-12. In one word, describe how Jesus' voice sounded to you as he spoke to his disciples. _____

Read Matthew 26:36-40. Jesus had reached the crisis point in his life and found his friends had gone to sleep on him. In one word, how do you think he felt? _____

Jesus was intent on his mission. He had called together certain people to be part of his ministry, and in his human nature he expected more understanding, better attention to his teaching, and more compassion for his pain. He, too, felt stress over these sorts of disappointment.

Read John 13:21-30. In this passage Jesus does not seem stressed by Judas' betrayal, even though it was far worse than any other disappointments Jesus had experienced up to that time. What is your opinion of this contrast?

_____

_____

_____

_____

_____

Perhaps Jesus expected more from his other disciples than he did from Judas; therefore he was disappointed in their responses. In a similar way we often feel stressed because of the unfulfilled expectations we have for ourselves and others. We automatically carry around many expectations and don't even realize that we have them until they go unfulfilled. It's a human tendency to assume that our expectations will be fulfilled; therefore, we often get bent out of shape when expectations *aren't* fulfilled.

Ponder: When were your reasonable expectations not met? How did you feel?

The Stress of Jockeying for Control

One of the biggest contributions to a life of too much stress is living under someone else's control. It could be a parent, parent-in-law, spouse, neighbor, pastor, boss, or (and this is common) a child or teenager who has somehow obtained control of your home and your life. Many controllers are not ogres but are friendly, pleasant people (as long as they get their own way). They control with money, criticism, lack of praise, silence, rejection, and sometimes extreme kindness.

If you feel controlled, write about your situation here.

_____

_____

_____

_____

_____

_____

Trying to control your spouse, children, or friends also takes its toll on your body. You can control anyone for a while, but if a person continuously struggles to get away from you — and teenagers are quite creative in their struggles for independence — it takes great energy to hang on. If you tend to be someone who "hangs on," consider this: Is this the way you want to use your energy? Controlling people's lives, making their decisions, and feeling guilt for their failures? If this touches a raw spot in your life, write about it here.

_____

_____

_____

_____

_____

_____

Read Psalm 44:9-22. This psalm is the cry of a people living under the stress of captivity — the stress of others *controlling* them.

The Stress of Parenthood

Parenthood and stress go hand in hand. Often it's the child who gives parents the greatest joy who also causes the greatest stress. Parents feel such turmoil because they care so much about their children. If you are a parent, what is the most exhausting and/or stressful time of parenting that you've endured?

_____

_____

_____

_____

_____

_____

The Stress of Being Single
and Living Alone

For many people the single life is a lonely life. Singles have so much affection to give and have so much need for affection. Yet there is often no one to meet their needs. The lonely single person longs for simple activities that the rest of the population takes for granted. Something as simple as coming home from work and sitting down at the kitchen table to talk with a spouse or other family member about the day is alien and precious to the lonely single person. Is loneliness a stress for you? If so, write about it here.

_____

_____

_____

_____

Being single and female can mean even more stress. If you're unmechanical, simple things like a car quitting, a roof leaking, a furnace going out, or a sewer backing up can cause major problems. It is so nice to have someone fix things without worrying about whether he or she (a) is competent, (b) charges a fair price, and (c) behaves politely and professionally.

Being single and female can also be frightening because you worry about things like entering your apartment alone at night, mysterious phone calls with "nobody" on the other end, your male neighbor across the hall who often comes home drunk and disorderly, or a landlord who refuses to install better locks on your doors. Sometimes it's easy to envy women who don't have these kinds of struggles. If you're single, female, and live alone, write your feelings about this.

_____

_____

_____

_____

_____

_____

The Stress of Illness

Dealing with your own or someone else's physical pain is stressful, even if it does help you mature. This is also true of having to deal with the chronically ill, including an alcoholic or drug-dependent parent, spouse, or child. Coping with the long drawn-out problems associated with someone's Alzheimer's disease, birth defects, minimal brain damage, or dyslexia leaves many people physically and emotionally exhausted. In the Bible, Job is the classic figure we can look to in order to see a person of faith struggling with physical hardship. Your own physical limitations such as arthritis, premenstrual syndrome, prostate problems, menopause, or any of countless other maladies are all stressful. Are any of these physical problems something that you have to deal with? If so, write about it here.

_____

_____

_____

_____

_____

The Stress of Expecting Too Much
From Yourself

Often the people who get overstressed are the ones who tend to be the most reliable, most faithful, and the hardest working. Usually, they were the oldest or only children in their families of origin. They are the ones most likely to expect too much of themselves. If you are an oldest or only child, you started out in life developing ahead of most babies because you had your parents' sole attention. Your proud parents kept expecting you to perform better than other children. Given this situation, most oldest and only children, even as adults, continue to expect more of themselves long after their parents' goals for them have been reached.

If you, or someone who loves you, expects more from you than you feel you can give, write about it here.

_____

_____

_____

_____

If you have written something in the space above, this may be the greatest reason you feel so much stress in your body.

Read about Martha and Mary (Luke 10:38-42) to see what Jesus had to say about being overstressed.

The Stress of Problems That Have No Solutions

Joe grew up where the seasons of the year were definite, and now he lives in a region where it's always summer. He feels frustrated, but there is no way to return "home." Andrew is in love with a woman who treats him nicely but does not return his love. Toni has a boss who jumps from project to project while Toni, by nature, is a perfectionist who wants to finish one project before moving on to another. Georgeann grew up in a home where there was never a threat of turning off the electricity, and now her bills go unpaid to such an extent that she hates to answer the phone.

Read Genesis 27:34-38 to find a biblical example of someone who had to deal with the stress of a problem with no solution.

If there is a problem in your life that you can find no solution for, write about it here.

_____

_____

_____

_____

_____

_____

The Stress of Daily Hassles

Do you have to deal with consistent problems involving too much paperwork, personal disagreements, undone housecleaning, too many people asking for your time, late appointments, or broken appliances?

When Karen went in to the hospital for thirty days, her sister, Jean, volunteered to take care of Karen's toddler and keep house. Jean took a leave of absence from her full-time work in a mission where she served hungry and desperate men, women, and children. After she'd finished her stint, Jean said, "My month at Karen's house was the hardest work I've ever done."

Stan and Virginia were in the midst of adjusting to a second marriage when his two youngest and her two youngest, all in their early twenties, moved in with them. The "children" worked odd hours, made messes in the kitchen, hung on the phone, and instead of politely taking messages, they asked Stan's and Virginia's callers to ring back later.

Joanne said it was not her job that was difficult but all the interruptions and hassles on the job — unimportant phone calls, meetings that wasted time, people who wanted to talk about their vacations, someone borrowing a disk to her computer and not returning it.

Some researchers believe that a life of many minor hassles is more difficult than a life where the stresses are large but easily defined.

What are the daily hassles of your life?

_____

_____

_____

_____

_____

_____

_____

Steps to Take to Get a Handle on Your Stress

First, if possible, think of a sympathetic person who knows how to listen and call that person on the phone. Ask if you can have a few minutes of his or her time. Tell this person ahead of time, "I'm not calling you for advice. I just want you to listen to me." If this is a convenient time for the person to be on the phone, share what you have written in this lesson about the stresses of your life. It's really helpful to give voice to your problems. Just remember that this person's time is valuable too. Don't keep your friend on the phone too long, and don't get into the habit of calling your friend about every single problem in your life. Offer to listen to his or her problems too.

Second, using the material from lesson one about the way your body operates, consider how all the problem areas you wrote about in this lesson may affect the way your body functions. Here are some of the most common physical warnings that signal a life that's enduring too much stress:

- disturbed sleep,
- a wound-up feeling,
- muscle tightness and/or pain in your neck and shoulders,
- tightness in the pit of your stomach,
- headaches,
- difficulty in swallowing.

Are any of these symptoms yours? Do you see a correlation between them and what's going on in your life? In times of crisis, it's important that you don't add to your stress by trying to be brave because you are Christian. It's okay to admit that all is not well.

Read Acts 20:36-38. This is a mini-story about Saint Paul's farewell to the Ephesian elders. Do these people seem brave to you?_____

Are they pretending they are not sad?_____

Are they afraid of being a "bad example" if they cry? _____

_____

Read Luke 1:46-49. When Mary, the mother of Jesus, went to Elizabeth's house, Elizabeth exclaimed prophetically, "Blessed are you among women, and blessed is the fruit of your womb" (Luke 1:42). Then Mary burst into the words you just read that are so full of joy and promise.

Now read Luke 2:34-35. What is going to happen to Mary?

_____

_____

_____

_____

Judging from this prophecy, how do you think Mary felt as she watched her son die on the cross? Was she brave? Was she joyful? Of course not. She was sorrowful in the extreme.

Ponder: How *should* Christians think and act in times of stress or sorrow? What do the above Scriptures say to you about trying to be "brave"?

By now you are probably saying, "Okay, I see the problem. But where are the solutions?" They're coming next. During the following eight weeks you will have a great deal of enjoyment finding the answers. You'll decide on things like priorities, how much energy you have to spare (if any), how to take care of *you,* how to say NO, when to pray, and even new ways to pray. The tools you gain will last a lifetime.

Wrap Up

Gaining control: On page 140 fill in the *I-Gain-Control-of-My-Life Chart* for lesson four.

Continue during the week: This week recall three situations involving continuing stress when you felt you had to behave like a "strong, brave Christian." Then go back and talk to a person who saw you in that strong and brave mode. Ask this person what he or she thinks would have happened if you had instead admitted you were having a hard time and needed help.

Just for fun: Unplug the phone. Take a long bubble bath. If bubble baths aren't your style, find a hot tub, whirlpool, or Jacuzzi, and spend some time in it.

Journal experience: Write about the most painful time of your life. Write about how you think Jesus would respond to your pain.

Memorize: "We are children of God, and if children, then heirs, heirs of God and joint heirs with Christ, if only we suffer with him so that we may also be glorified with him" (Romans 8:16-17).

Weekly log exercise: List below the continuing stresses you face during the coming week. As they come to mind, include as many stresses from the past as you can remember if they add to your stress today.

Day 1 _____

_____

_____

Day 2 _____

_____

_____

Day 3 _____

_____

_____

Day 4 _____

_____

_____

Day 5 _____

_____

_____

Day 6 _____

_____

_____

Day 7 _____

_____

_____

Closing prayer:

Dear Lord, I'm glad that I don't have to be brave about the continuing stress of my life.

Glory be to the Father, and to the Son, and to the Holy Spirit, as it was in the beginning, is now, and ever shall be, world without end. Amen.

PART TWO:
Finding
Solutions

Lesson Five
Setting Priorities

Beginning prayer:

Dear God, please help me allow you to paint my life in the colors that are most pleasing to you.

Glory be to the Father, and to the Son, and to the Holy Spirit, as it was in the beginning, is now, and ever shall be, world without end. Amen.

The Lesson: Figuring Out What's Really Important (and What's Not)

It was one of those times when I could feel the buildup of stress in my body. I felt too tired, too hungry, and too irritated by everyone. Everything I could think of to do sounded too difficult or too boring or too purposeless. After two days of this, I said to myself, "Okay, Pat, I think you're overstressed. What's going on that's too much for you to handle?" I sat down at my desk and wrote at the top of the page, *What's bothering me?* Underneath I wrote:

1. Bill's continuing heart problem following his surgery;
2. A function I don't want to attend;
3. A recent failure;
4. An important book-writing project.

I looked over my list, and it didn't seem too overwhelming, except for the last item. Maybe I was feeling more pushed by it than I realized. It's so easy to add a task here and a task there until the load gets to be too much. So I made a second heading for a list and wrote *Priorities*. It was an easy list to make because I've done it so often that I know what my priorities are. As I wrote it out, I saw what I would have to do. The "important" book-writing project would have to go. I was working on it with a friend but decided that even if it meant disappointing a lot of people, and even if it meant something worthwhile would not get done, I could not go on with the project. That writing task, when looked at in relationship to my priorities, wasn't as important for me to do as it seemed. Even though my body rebelled against the writing project, I don't think I could have seen it so clearly if I hadn't given it its rightful place on the priority list. I prayed about it, talked to Bill about it, and eventually picked up the phone and said to my friend, "I'm taking a six-month leave of absence from our project." Even though my friend found my decision hard to take, I felt like a freed person as soon as I had made the call. The stress of having more than I could do was off, and it felt so good to be rid of it.

What Are Your Priorities?

To understand your first priority, **read Deuteronomy 6:5.** In this passage we are commanded to _____

_____

In order to love God, we need to know him. We come to know God by spending time with him.

Read Jeremiah 29:13-14. How are we to seek the Lord?

_____

_____

Ponder: What do you think it means to seek the Lord with all your heart?

Read 1 Peter 2:9. We belong to God so that we can _____ him. We are a _____ race or people. We are a _____ priesthood. We are a _____ nation. We are a people who _____ to God. Yes, God has indeed called us out of darkness and into light!

Read 1 John 1:9. God _____ our sins.

Read Jeremiah 31:3. Write here exactly what God is saying through the prophet Jeremiah.

_____

_____

_____

_____

Read Romans 5:8. To show his love, _____ died for us.

Now, using the above Scriptures, write why you would want to make daily time with God your first priority.

_____

_____

_____

_____

_____

Share what you have written with a good friend.

If you're married, read Genesis 2:24, Matthew 19:4-6, and Ephesians 5:31 to find out how marriage fits in with your priorities. In these passages, who are married couples directed to cling to?

_____

If you have been called by God to be one flesh with your spouse, is anyone, other than God, more important to you than your spouse?

_____

_____

If you have children, who is more important to you, your children or your spouse?

_____

How do you feel about your answers to these questions? Is there anything you'd like to change?

_____

_____

On the day that I made out my list of priorities, I wrote:
1. Jesus is first.
2. Bill needs me.
3. The children need me. (There were two left at home and a constant welcome stream of adult children and grand-children.)
4. My mother needs me.
5. *I* need me, with quality time for reading, relaxing, and walking.
6. My prayer group and I need one another (half day a week).
7. I'm writing the study book on stress.
8. I want to teach and speak (one day a week).
9. Cooking, shopping, laundry, cleaning.

Now you can see why the "important" writing project was overwhelming me on a subconscious level, even though I had the talent for it and a strong interest in it.

Setting Your Own Priorities

In the left-hand column below, make a list of all the activities that take your time. Use another sheet of paper, if necessary. You can make your list in one of two ways: (1) Exclude your paid job and prioritize everything else or (2) place your paid job, especially if you have irregular hours, within your priorities. Write down anything that comes to mind. In the right-hand column prioritize them according to the importance you want to give them in your life. Rank them on a scale that uses "1" for most important, "2" for second most important, and so on.

Activity	Priority Ranking
_____	_____
_____	_____
_____	_____
_____	_____
_____	_____
_____	_____
_____	_____
_____	_____

A prioritized list is like a road map for your life. Look at this "road map" and draw a serious or funny "map" of what your life looks like. When you've finished, share your drawing with a friend.

Wrap Up

Gaining control: On page 140 fill in the *I-Gain-Control-of-My-Life Chart* for lesson five.

Continue during the week: This week continue adding to and/or subtracting from your priorities list. After you add and/or subtract, be sure to relabel each priority with an importance rating from the one-to-ten scale. This activity will prepare you for the next lesson.

Just for fun: Eat something zany for breakfast one day this coming week — something like popcorn or the latest multicolored cereal for kids.

Journal experience: Write a letter to yourself from God, addressing what you think the Lord might have to say about your life. Feel the Holy Spirit inspiring you as you do this.

Memorize: Write out the following segment of Psalm 91, which speaks of security under God's protection. Tape it to your bathroom mirror, over the kitchen sink, or anywhere that will help you memorize it.

I will set him on high because he acknowledges my name.
He shall call upon me, and I will answer him;
I will be with him in distress;
I will deliver him and glorify him;
with length of days I will gratify him
and will show him my salvation.
(Psalm 91:14-16)

Closing prayer:

Dear God, thank you for your wonderful and colorful plan for my life.

Glory be to the Father, and to the Son, and to the Holy Spirit, as it was in the beginning, is now, and ever shall be, world without end. Amen.

Lesson Six
The Eight-Part Plan for Taking Care of Your Body

Beginning prayer:
Dear God, show me the ways I can be a Good Samaritan to myself.

Glory be to the Father, and to the Son, and to the Holy Spirit, as it was in the beginning, is now, and ever shall be, world without end. Amen.

The Lesson: Taking Care of Yourself

This is your creative opportunity to take a familiar piece of Scripture — the parable of The Good Samaritan (Luke 10:29-37) — and relate it to the stress in your life. Fill in the blanks below with your words. The ways I would fill in the words are at the end of the chapter, but yours may very well be more creative.

You were going down (1) _____

when you fell into the hands of stressors. They stripped you of

your (2)_____ and left you (3) _____

and (4) _____.

A priest, who was in reality the religious part of you, saw you lying there all (5) _____ and _____ and said, "This poor person has (6) _____. I'll remember to pray for this unfortunate one at church."

Then a Levite, who was in reality the performing part of you, came by and said, "This poor character really looks all (7) ____ _____, but I know that (s)he can get up if (s)he wants to, after all, where there's a will there's a way." The Levite hurried on to a (8) _____.

Next came a Samaritan. The Samaritan was in reality the sympathetic part of your psyche and not too well thought of by the religious and performing parts. The Samaritan came by and saw how totally (9) _____ you were. This Samaritan (10) _____ all plans for the time being and (11) _____ your wounds as you lay there, injured. The Samaritan poured on the oil of (12) _____ and the wine of (13) _____. Then the Samaritan saw to it that you had a (14) _____ where you could (15) _____. The Samaritan promised to pay whatever it cost to see you well again.

Jesus asked, "Which of these was a neighbor to the one who had fallen into the hands of stressors?"

The answer was, "The one who had mercy."

Jesus said, "Go and do likewise."

When You Need a Good Samaritan

When you see yourself as an exhausted victim of too much stress, then you know that Jesus would have you stop in the middle of your journey, care for your wounds, and rest until you are better. For a season of your life, you may have to be a Good Samaritan to yourself.

One morning, as I was planning for this lesson, the phone rang and my neighbor Sandi said, "A woman in my study group has a message for you. After hearing you speak on being a Good Samaritan to yourself, she began following your Eight-Part Plan to take care of herself physically. That plan and praying is what got her through one of the most stressful times of her life."

The basis of this plan is found at the end of a fascinating story in Scripture. Elijah had presided over a huge spectacular at Mount Carmel where he called down fire from heaven to consume offerings soaked with water. He did this in order to show that *God* was the true God, not Baal, whom many of the people had been worshiping. God then consumed the offering with fire. When this happened, Jezebel became so angry with Elijah that she threatened to kill him. Elijah ran for his life until he was so exhausted he stopped and fell asleep under a tree after begging God to let him die. (See 1 Kings 18:16-46—19:1-5.)

Elijah sounds like many of us. We can get all involved with the projects the Lord has for us. But when they are done, we run in another direction until we are so exhausted that, given a chance, we'd be happy to fall asleep under a tree.

Read what happened next to Elijah in 1 Kings 19:5-6. What did the angel provide for Elijah? _____

Read 1 Kings 19:7-8. Why did the angel insist that Elijah eat again?

_____

What are your personal thoughts about the advantages of a hot meal? _____

Sustenance in the face of challenges is one of the most important reasons why we must take care of our bodies — so that the journey ahead will not be too difficult.

Read Mark 5:35-43. What did Jesus say to the parents of the child whom he raised from the dead? _____

_____

What do you think of this advice?

_____

_____

_____

_____

_____

Read Matthew 15:32-37. What was Jesus' concern?

_____

_____

_____

_____

What did he do? _____

On a scale of 1 to 10 (with 1 meaning "very well"), how well do you pay attention to the proper nourishment of your body? ____

Read Mark 6:30-33. What's going on in this passage?

_____

_____

_____

What did Jesus tell his disciples to do?

_____

_____

_____

This passage shows that we, in our day and age, aren't the only ones who have led busy lives. What does this passage say to you?

_____

_____

_____

_____

_____

_____

Read Isaiah 28:11-13. In this passage, God provides _____

_____. But the people would not _____ .

As a result, what happened to them?

_____

_____

_____

_____

This passage contains a warning to those who keep on and on and on and do not rest.

Ponder: Can you think of a time when God provided rest for you, and you did not take it? What happened as a result?

Read Exodus 23:12, 31:15, 34:21, and 35:2. Then read Leviticus 23:3. What is God's instruction in these passages?

_____

_____

_____

_____

Why do you think Scripture gives this same advice five times?

_____

_____

_____

_____

The constant message in all of the Scripture passages you've just read is that God is concerned with your physical well-being. He sent an angel to feed Elijah, he provided food for the hungry crowds, he commanded physical rest for his people, and he sought a place of rest for his disciples.

Rhyming exercise: Finish the following sentence using words that rhyme. *If we do not take care of our bodies, they will*

_____ *and* _____ . (Example: *stop and drop*).

The Eight-Part Plan

Step 1. *See a doctor.* Go once a year if you are over fifty, once every two years if you are under fifty. You probably need some routine tests done anyway. If you have any distressing symptoms, tell them to your doctor. It's okay to have physical needs, even if you're a wonderful Christian. When was your last physical exam?

_____

Step 2. *Take stress vitamins daily.* When you're under stress, your body needs extra vitamin C and more B vitamins than your food can provide. How much vitamin C does your present vitamin supplement give you? _____ Ask your doctor or consult a reliable source to see if that is enough.

Step 3. *Cut caffeine to three cups of coffee, tea, or cola a day.* Contrary to popular opinion, caffeine actually *destroys* your energy by giving you a false (and addictive) high. Urging on a tired body with a cup of coffee is a bit like whipping a weary horse struggling with a heavy load. On average, how many servings of caffeine are you presently drinking each day?

_____

Step 4. *Eat right.* Include the four basic food groups in your daily diet. Use the "4-4-2-2 plan" for each day. That means you need four servings of fruits and/or vegetables, four servings of grain products, two servings from the meat group (this includes legumes such as peanut butter and soybeans), and two servings of dairy products.

On the next page, write out what you had to eat yesterday.

Breakfast _____

_____

_____

Lunch _____

_____

_____

Dinner _____

_____

_____

Any snacks _____

_____

_____

Now, circle the fruits and vegetables in blue, the grains in green, meat groups in red, and the dairy products in yellow. Circle anything made mostly of sugar in black!

Now, write out a sample menu for you that will nourish your body and give you strength for the week ahead. Use different colored inks as you did above. I've filled in the first day for you as an example.

DAY 1

Breakfast: Egg, whole-wheat toast, orange juice.
Lunch: Cheese sandwich on rye, low-fat milk, carrot sticks. (For every carrot stick I eat, I treat myself to a potato chip.)
Dinner: Baked chicken, broccoli, coleslaw, rice, low-fat milk.
Snacks: Rice crackers, yogurt, fruit.

DAY 2

Breakfast: _____

Lunch: _____

_____

Dinner: _____

_____

Snacks: _____

DAY 3

Breakfast: _____

Lunch: _____

_____

Dinner: _____

_____

Snacks: _____

DAY 4

Breakfast: _____

Lunch: _____

_____

Dinner: _____

_____

Snacks: _____

DAY 5

Breakfast: _____

Lunch: _____

_____

Dinner: _____

_____

Snacks: _____

DAY 6

Breakfast: _____

Lunch: _____

_____

Dinner: _____

_____

Snacks: _____

DAY 7

Breakfast: _____

Lunch: _____

_____

Dinner: _____

_____

Snacks: _____

Step 5. *Get enough rest.* Go to bed without watching the news on television. People whose lives are stressful may need as much as ten hours of sleep a night. How many hours of sleep do you get a night? _____

Step 6. *Exercise daily.* Brisk walking is one of the best forms of exercise. Exercise helps maintain bone strength, enhances heart and lung functioning, improves skin tone, and helps the body absorb nutrients. My walks are a great source of enjoyment to me. One day I counted all the colors of green I could see. Some days I talk with my friend Jesus. Sometimes it's on my walk that a solution to a problem pops into my head. My husband, Bill, solves some of his most perplexing problems during his daily two-mile walk. When I'm walking, I sometimes empty my mind of all lofty thoughts and just enjoy the strength of the wind or the warmth of the sun on my skin. I always return home refreshed. Do you exercise daily? _____ If not, how often *do* you exercise?

_____

If you're not happy with your answers about exercise, write down here what step or steps you will take in the next week to improve your exercise habits.

_____

_____

_____

_____

_____

Step 7. *Have fun.* What's really fun for you? One day I asked the Lord to be in charge of my fun. Later, I heard an inner voice urging me to go to the beach and look at the sunset. I replied,

"No, I have to clean the mold off the bathroom tile." The voice urged me more, but getting that mold off seemed so important. Again, the voice came and insisted that I put my spray bottle and towel on the table and walk out the door toward the beach. So I did. It was a picture-postcard evening. The sunset filled the sky as if it were peach and orange and raspberry parfait layered in a vast bowl. The tide thrashed the beach, and the gulls cried out to the fishermen. I stood there drinking in salt air and music and beauty like the thirsting traveler I was. I thought of how I'd almost missed the exquisite fun of this mini-adventure because of some mold on the bathroom tile that didn't matter at all. When was the last time you did something that was fun?

_____

What was it?

_____

_____

_____

Step 8. *Relax.* There are a lot of ways to relax the tensions out of your body, but here is my favorite. For this you need to have a partner. Each person should take a turn giving the other a foot massage. Here are the steps to follow:

a. Put a little oil or lotion on the foot and softly rub it in.
b. Gently massage and rub each toe and then give each one a little tug.
c. Rub your thumb up and down the bottom of the foot several times, beginning at the heel and working up toward the toes.
d. Massage the ball of the foot, then the top.
e. Hold the foot gently and rotate the ankle.
f. End with a little tug on the leg.
g. Repeat steps a. through f. on the other foot.

What do *you* do to relax on a regular basis? _____

_____

_____

_____

If you're not doing enough relaxing, review the priorities you drew up in chapter five. What can you cut from your life to make room for you to be a Good Samaritan to yourself?

_____

_____

_____

Wrap Up

Gaining control: On page 140 fill in the *I-Gain-Control-of-My-Life Chart* for lesson six.

Continue during the week: The Eight-Part Plan takes time. A little more time for eating, sleeping longer, exercising, having fun, and relaxing will take an extra hour from each day. For many people this extra time is not an option. However, life has so many stresses for you that the Eight-Part Plan is now a necessity, not an option. If you feel all eight steps are too much for you to deal with right now, start gradually with one or two. Decide which of the eight is/are the most important to your well-being. As you carry out the steps you choose to follow, see what difference you notice.

Just for fun: Fix yourself a pleasant breakfast on a tray and take it back to bed. If that isn't your cup of tea, invite *one* friend (more than one is too stressful) over and barbecue hamburgers.

Journal experience: Ask God to be the recreation and leisure director of your life. Record how you think God would respond to this request.

Memorize: "For six days you may work, but on the seventh day you shall rest; on that day you must rest even during the seasons of plowing and harvesting" (Exodus 34:21).

Closing prayer:
Thank you God for your beautiful world. Please forgive me for not taking time to enjoy it more.

Glory be to the Father, and to the Son, and to the Holy Spirit, as it was in the beginning, is now, and ever shall be, world without end. Amen.

Possible answers to Good Samaritan puzzle: (1) the road of life, (2) energy, (3) wounded, (4) totally exhausted, (5) hurting and weary, (6) a spiritual problem, (7) worn out, (8) committee meeting, (9) burned out, (10) canceled, (11) bandaged, (12) compassion, (13) nurturing, (14) place, (15) rest.

Lesson Seven
Energy Levels

Beginning prayer:
Dear God, please give me eyes to see where my energy is being spent.

Glory be to the Father, and to the Son, and to the Holy Spirit, as it was in the beginning, is now, and ever shall be, world without end. Amen.

The Lesson:
Preventing a Personal Energy Crisis

Carrying around too much stress is to our bodies what overspending is to our pocketbooks. If you had charged your limit on three credit cards, the money in the bank was completely gone, and there was only ten dollars a day to live on, you would have to make some choices about what you would buy. If you were a responsible person (which I'm sure you are), you'd tell yourself, "No extras until the charge cards are paid off and the money builds up again!"

Likewise, when we've used up all our energy through hauling around too much stress, we have to make some choices about what we will spend our energy on. No extras until the energy builds up again! (And it often builds up slower than money does!)

So we have to be stricter with our energy than we are with our money. We already know how to go to the store and only spend what we need to get by on until payday. If we spend it all in the bakery department, then we won't have any left for eggs and produce. So most of us make a grocery list and cut out everything we don't really need.

In the same way, we need to learn to go through the day spending only the energy we can afford for that day. If we try to spend more than we have, we will end up neglecting the important things. All of this is easy to say and hard to do. Cutting out activities is difficult. You may have been "Superwoman" or "Superman" for so long that being ordinary does not feel all that comfortable. You may be thinking, *I've always done things this way. I've always been "wonderful" or at least attempted it.* So how do we stop and realistically live so we are not burning out our bodies to the point that we become ineffectual? One good way to accomplish this is to plan ahead.

Read Luke 14:28-30. What is Jesus' advice to the one who wants to build a tower? The person should _____ to see if there is enough _____ . If the person doesn't do this he will _____ _____ to finish.

Read Luke 14:31-32. In this hypothetical example, what should a king do before he goes to war? He is to sit down first and ____ _____ if he has enough _____ to fight the enemy.

How would you apply this to your life? _____
_____
_____

Read Proverbs 6:6-8. The ant is being commended because in storing her provisions she is_____

Read Proverbs 22:3. The shrewd man _____ for the future while those who don't _____

Read Proverbs 24:27. Here is similar advice that basically tells us to _____

_____

_____

What kind of suffering do you think will come to the person who is already weary and overburdened yet doesn't plan ahead?

_____

_____

_____

_____

It's planning ahead, not desiring to please people or performing or succeeding that must determine how you decide to act. This lesson will help you make some important decisions about planning by showing you how many energy tickets you have to spend each day. With this knowledge you can plan ahead and reduce the stress levels of your life.

As a result of doing this lesson myself, I decided not to have my son's music teachers and their families over for dinner. I would have loved inviting them, but I would have added far more stress to my life than I would have reaped in enjoyment.

The Social Readjustment Rating Scale

Thomas H. Holmes, a psychiatrist at the University of Washington School of Medicine, developed the following Social Readjustment Rating Scale (*Journal of Psychosomatic Research,* 11:213-218, 1967, Pergamon Press, Inc.). He warns that if several items on the list occur with intensity and close to the same time, they will create an unfavorable life situation. His list ends with minor violations of the law. I have added some further stress points and have left it for you to determine their degree of impact (number) on your life.

Use your sum total of points as a warning beacon. If 300 points of stress — or even close to that — are occurring in your life, you need to drastically readjust your lifestyle to compensate for the loss of emotional energy you have sustained.

STRESS	POINTS
Death of spouse	100
Divorce	73
Marital separation from mate	65
Detention in jail or other institution	63
Death of a close family member	63
Major personal injury or illness	53
Marriage	50
Being fired at work	47
Marital reconciliation with mate	45
Retirement from work	45
Major change in the health or behavior of a family member	44
Pregnancy	40
Sexual difficulties	39
Gaining a new family member (through birth, adoption, older person moving in, etc.)	39
Major business readjustment (merger, reorganization, bankruptcy, etc.)	39

Major change in financial state (a lot worse off or a lot better off than usual)	38
Death of a close friend	37
Changing to a different line of work	36
Major change in the number of arguments with spouse (either a lot more or a lot less than usual regarding child-rearing, personal habits, etc.)	35
Taking out a mortgage or loan for a major purchase (for a home, business, etc.)	31
Foreclosure on a mortgage or loan	30
Major change in responsibilities at work (promotion, demotion, lateral transfer)	29
Son or daughter leaving home (marriage, attending college, etc.)	29
Trouble with in-laws	29
Outstanding personal achievement	28
Wife beginning or ceasing work outside the home	26
Beginning or ceasing formal schooling	26
Major change in living conditions (building a new home, remodeling, deterioration of home or neighborhood)	25
Revision of personal habits (dress, manners, associations, etc.)	24
Trouble with the boss	23
Major change in working hours or conditions	20
Change in residence	20
Changing to a new school	20
Major change in usual type and/or amount of recreation	19
Major change in church activities (a lot more or a lot less than usual)	19
Major change in social activities (clubs, dancing, movies, visiting, etc.)	18
Taking out a mortgage or loan for a lesser purchase (for a car, TV, freezer, etc.)	17
Major change in sleeping habits (a lot more or a lot less sleep, or a change in part of day when asleep)	16

Major change in number of family get-togethers (a lot more or a lot less than usual)	15
Major change in eating habits (a lot more or a lot less food intake, or very different meal hours or surroundings)	15
Vacation	13
Christmas	12
Minor violations of the law (traffic tickets, jaywalking, disturbing the peace, etc.)	11

Additional Stresses

Pain in child or grandchild's life
Trouble in child or grandchild's life
Handicap or sickness of someone in your care
Unconfessed major sin
Being a crime victim
Unforgiveness, bitterness, resentment
Remarriage
Remarriage with children involved
Marriage to an alcoholic/drug-dependent person
Your own alcohol/drug dependence
Being single and living alone
Extra people in your home (including adult children)
Loving someone who does not love you
Not loving someone who does love you
Living in a controlled situation
Working in a controlled situation
Not having time for yourself
Trouble in your church
A feeling of not being good enough
Not being appreciated
Not being understood
Not being needed

How did you do? If your score was 275 or higher, write here what changes you want to make in your life to help lower that score.

_____

_____

_____

_____

It would be good to take this test about four times every year. It will help you keep in touch with your life and keep it from careening out of control.

Wrap Up

Gaining control: On page 140 fill in the *I-Gain-Control-of-My-Life Chart* for lesson seven.

Continue during the week: The best way to learn something is to teach it. Find a time this week with your spouse or a good friend and help him/her go through the Social Readjustment Rating Scale. Discuss his/her possible life changes as a result of the test.

Just for fun: Do something you've always wanted to do but were too cautious to try. (*Warning:* Don't do anything crazy that could stress you even more, like throwing a big party.)

Journal experience: If you scored higher than 275 on the Social Readjustment Rating Scale, write down what item on the scale scored highest for you. Then write about what's so difficult about that event and how the difficulty got started. If, after taking this test, you feel that you have sufficient energy to take on something new, write out what you would like to do. Tell yourself *why* you would like to do it. Ask the Lord if you are trying to impress someone else with this choice or if you are honestly doing it for the joy of it. Record God's answer.

Memorize:

By wisdom is a house built,
    by understanding is it made firm;
And by knowledge are its rooms filled
    with every precious and pleasing possession.

(Proverbs 24:3-4)

Closing prayer:

Dear God, thank you for letting me see the source of my stress and energy problems. Please help me now with the solutions.

Glory be to the Father, and to the Son, and to the Holy Spirit, as it was in the beginning, is now, and ever shall be, world without end. Amen.

Lesson Eight
The Importance
of Saying No

Beginning prayer:
Dear God, teach me your ways and protect me from mine.
Glory be to the Father, and to the Son, and to the Holy Spirit,
as it was in the beginning, is now, and ever shall be, world
without end. Amen.

The Lesson:
Why We Say Yes and How to Change

To reduce stress we need to identify our reasons for helping others. We tend to do

- the wrong thing for the wrong reason.
- the wrong thing for the right reason.
- the right thing for the wrong reason.
- the right thing for the right reason.

Of course we'd all like to fit into that last category, but let's look at the other three first.

Doing the wrong thing for the wrong reason: An example of this might be trying to control people's lives so you can feel important. Or it could mean making yourself indispensable so others won't leave you.

Doing the wrong thing for the right reason: This could mean something like divulging someone else's confidential information because you want prayer for him or her. Or it could be leaving your teenagers unsupervised for the weekend because you need to get away.

Doing the right thing for the wrong reason: Included here are things like volunteering at school or church so you can feel like a good person or saying yes to other people's needs in order to be liked by them. It is a much harder thing to see clearly when you are doing the right thing for the wrong reason. Some people are "performance oriented." That means they have to perform in order to feel good about themselves. Often, although not always, people who are the oldest children in their families suffer with performance orientation. They often had to take on a lot of responsibility at an early age, and when they did, their contribution was judged as valuable. As a result, these oldest children have often heard from their parents and others that it was *them* (not their contribution) that was valuable when they performed. So they performed again, took responsibility again and again, and came to feel more and more valuable. The problem with this cycle is that these people usually come to the point where they believe that if they aren't performing, they are no good. Therefore, the way they see themselves has become tied to what they accomplish.

If this sounds like you, the scene is set for you to do the right (generous, helpful, responsible) thing for the wrong reason, which is to feel good about yourself. If you keep doing this, the stress will mount as you work harder and harder. If a child, spouse, or friend disappoints you, *you* feel like a failure. If your project fails, *you* feel you have failed, not the project. However, instead of reaching for a drink or a drug, as someone else might do, you make up for your failure feelings by adding to your workload. While other people are out there destroying their bodies with substance abuse, in a similar way you are too, if you are very performance oriented.

Even if you do right things for the right reasons, this can turn on you as more and more people need your help, and it seems there is no one else to carry the burden. Then the draining demands of people and their problems become too much. Suddenly, you realize there is no joy in your work, that you're the only one who cares, and you don't want to do it anymore. You started out right but never set limits to what you could do because no one else would help. That means that you ended up doing the right thing but for the wrong reason.

Doing the right thing for the right reason: Obviously, doing the right thing for the right reason is not as easy as it sounds. It depends on how much stress you have in your life (lesson seven), your priorities (lesson five), your underlying motives, and your ability to say no.

What Scripture Has to Say

Let's look at some facts from the Bible.

Read Psalm 8:5-6. When God made you, what did he crown you with? _____

Do you deserve honor and glory? _____ Do you have to earn it? _____ Why do you think God crowned you with it? _____

_____

Read Psalm 139:13-14. God _____ you together and his works are _____.

Why are you wonderful?

_____

_____

_____

Is being made by God enough to be a wonderful person?

_____

The Scriptures explicitly state that we are wonderful because of God's handiwork. God doesn't expect your performance to improve on his work.

Read Psalm 40:9. What should your motive be?

_____

How do you think God's will for what you do might differ from your will?

_____

_____

_____

What, specifically, do you feel God wants for you?

_____

_____

_____

What, specifically, do you feel _you_ want for you?

_____

_____

_____

Read Ecclesiastes 3:13. God's _____ to us is that we find _____ in our labor. Work is good. Accomplishing our tasks feels good. God's gift to us is the satisfaction of a job well done, not any praise we get (or don't get) from others.

How would you explain the difference between the *satisfaction* of work and the *need* to work in order to feel like a worthwhile person?

_____

_____

_____

There are many "good" things people will ask you to do. However, not all of them will be satisfying. Indeed, they may only burden you until you are exhausted. Let's look at how Jesus dealt with this problem. Remember that his active ministry lasted for only three years and that his top priority was to save the lost sheep of Israel — the Jews.

Read Luke 12:13-15. A man in the crowd has recognized Jesus' ability to judge correctly. Now he wants to take advantage of Jesus' talent. What does he want Jesus to do?

_____

_____

Why do you think Jesus refused to use his gift to settle this man's problems?

_____

_____

_____

_____

Read John 2:18-21 and John 6:30-59. What did the people ask of Jesus in these passages? _____ Boiled down to one word, what was Jesus' answer in both situations? _____

Read John 6:14-15. The people recognized Jesus as a prophet and wanted to make him a king (automatic head of the committee). How did he react to this?

_____

_____

_____

Why do you think Jesus didn't want to be made king?

_____

_____

_____

_____

As king, Jesus could have done good things for his people, but earthly kingship wasn't the will of his Father. What does Jesus' refusal to become the head of an earthly kingdom say to you?

_____

_____

_____

_____

_____

_____

Read Luke 6:1-11, 13:10-16, and John 5:1-17. In these passages Jesus rejects (says no to) some rigid rules. Paraphrase his words in contemporary language.

Luke 6:5 _____

_____

Luke 6:9 _____

_____

Luke 13:16 _____

_____

John 5:17 _____

_____

What are the rules that other people have made or have tried to make for your life?

_____

_____

_____

_____

People often make rules to control your life and make you bend to their wishes. Rules most often benefit rule-makers, but they do not always benefit those who are required to follow the rules.

When Other People Control Your Life

One of the great causes of stress for people is not having control of their lives. A good way to counteract the pressure of a stress-filled life is to establish one area of your life where you have complete control. If there are people in your life who have been dictators for a long time, saying no to these people will take a great deal of courage. That means you will have to make some changes. The results are worth all the effort and energy.

Whom do you have the hardest time saying no to?

_____

Why do you think this person is so hard to turn down?

_____

_____

_____

_____

Write out the way you will say no to this person in order to give yourself some control of your life.

_____

_____

_____

_____

It's quite possible that the person who is hardest on you is someone very close. In my own life there was one person I had a terrible time saying no to. Every day she planned more for me to do than I could physically accomplish. I would tell her not to be so hard on me, but she always wanted her own way. One day I decided to set an alarm and told her that when it went off, I was through for the day, regardless of how much I got done. That little gimmick helped me at last say no to someone else's unreasonable demands and *yes* to my own needs.

Read Matthew 25:1-13. This parable is about five people who knew the right answer, even when threatened with guilt. What was the reply of the five wise virgins?

_____

_____

When I was a girl, those five virgins who did not share their oil seemed selfish to me. Looking at them from an adult point of view, I can understand why they are called wise. What is your point of view on this?

_____

_____

_____

_____

_____

Jesus said no when a request was against his Father's will for him. He said no because the opinions of people didn't matter when he knew what was best. Jesus told the story of the wise virgins who said no to emphasize the point that we must sometimes stand up for ourselves and say no when we try to follow God's will for our lives. It's all right for you and me to say no too. However, there exists in this world someone who wants us to say yes to every demand that comes our way.

Read Matthew 4:1-11. What is the devil trying to do in this passage?

_____

_____

_____

What are Jesus' responses?

_____

_____

_____

What is the final "clincher" that Jesus actually *shouts* at the devil to get rid of him?

_____

_____

_____

Remember this story whenever you feel that too many of other people's demands are crowding out what God has in mind for you to do.

What do you think would be one of the best tricks that the devil could use to keep you from doing God's will in your life?

_____

_____

_____

How has this trick worked in your life?

_____

_____

_____

Wrap Up

Gaining control: On page 140 fill in the *I-Gain-Control-of-My-Life Chart* for lesson eight.

Continue during the week: Look back over the priorities you assembled for yourself in lesson five. Then decide what obligation facing you now is not on your priority list. Plan to say NO to it this week.

Just for fun: Stand in front of the bathroom mirror. Make eye contact with yourself and practice the following ways of saying no:

- Smiling NO,
- I-mean-it NO,
- I'm-sorry-but-I-can't-come NO,
- NO-way NO.

Journal experience: Draw a picture of yourself using the extra time that saying no has created for you. Then write about what work is truly satisfying to you and why it is satisfying. Write out what work is not satisfying to you. Ask the Lord if you are doing it to make yourself feel like a worthwhile person. Record his response.

Memorize:
> I will instruct you and show you the way you should walk;
> I will counsel you, keeping my eye on you.
>
> (Psalm 32:8)

Closing prayer:
Dear God, thank you for the example of Jesus who showed me how to say no to people so that he could say yes to your will.

Glory be to the Father, and to the Son, and to the Holy Spirit, as it was in the beginning, is now, and ever shall be, world without end. Amen.

Lesson Nine
Friends, the Ultimate
Support System

Beginning prayer:

Dear God, thank you for creating me so that I need the friendships of others.

Glory be to the Father, and to the Son, and to the Holy Spirit, as it was in the beginning, is now, and ever shall be, world without end. Amen.

The Lesson: Asking for Help Can
Reduce Your Stress

Joe was four, Katy was two, Barbie (our foster child) was eighteen months old. At that time I also had six older children in school. I was taking a creative writing class at the community college, and I desperately needed time to write. But when? There was that one hour a day when the children napped, but it wasn't enough.

Enter my friend Virginia. Her problem was Chris, a son who was at the height of the "terrible twos." To say that Chris was a handful understates it immeasurably. His combination of hyper-activity and genius meant that at no time could Virginia let him out of her sight without dire consequences. Yet she needed to paint and wallpaper and sew curtains for her new home. So we struck a bargain. I took Chris from 7:00 a.m. to 5:00 p.m. on Tuesdays. Virginia took my three children from 8:00 a.m. to noon on Wednesdays. I don't believe she was ever a minute late bringing them back! She got her home decorated, and I found time to write. When that long winter was over, we were both, thanks to each other, still sane.

Time went by, and the friendship Virginia and I shared widened to include Zoanne, Bette, Fran, Kiti, and Terri. We met six or seven times a year to share a meal and pray for one another's needs. The hardest part was learning to be real with one another. We were all so used to being strong and brave; therefore we tended to put our guard up, pretending that Christian leaders don't have problems.

While we all wanted to be honest, I believe that I may have been the first one to break the ice. My son had recently been killed, and I spent almost our whole luncheon sobbing. No rejoicing that he was with the Lord, no thanking God for any divine plan…just horrible, noisy, unceasing sobs. My friends gathered around me, prayed, and told me it was all right to cry for as long as I wanted.

One day after that, I was home alone and I still couldn't deal with the sorrow. I didn't know what to do. I called Zoanne and asked, "Will you pray for me? I'm not coping." Zoanne, full of mercy, prayed over the phone with all her heart. Soon I felt wonderfully better. The next time when I felt I couldn't cope, I called Terri and then Bette and then Kiti. When I'd called the whole list, I started over again. I felt embarrassed to be so needy, and yet I knew I couldn't handle life's sorrows alone.

In time I grew well again, and at a luncheon gathering Bette prayed, "O God, thank you for letting us pray for Pat and be a part of her healing." In those words I understood I had not been a burden to my friends. Instead, my need had brought us all closer.

As the months went by, our gathering became a haven where everyone could share their mistakes, their children's difficulties, and their anger. We had become for one another a refuge where no one ever said, "When are you going to get your act together?" Later, when I heard Christian psychiatrist Frank Minirth say that one of the best ways to beat burnout is to have a support system of friends, I nodded in happy agreement.

Read Mark 1:17-20, Mark 2:14, and Luke 6:13-16. Write out the names of the men in Jesus' support group.

_____

_____

_____

How did this support group come together? Did Jesus wait for

them to ask if they could join? _____

Read Matthew 9:9-12, Matthew 26:14-16, and John 20:24-25.
Did Jesus choose only the cream of the crop? _____
Describe some of Jesus' choices.

_____

_____

_____

Look up the following Scriptures and write down some of the things that Jesus and his friends talked about.

Matthew 16:21 _____

Matthew 17:1-9 _____

Matthew 18:1-3 _____

Matthew 18:21 _____

Matthew 19:24-28 _____

Matthew 20:20-28 _____

Matthew 26:20-25 _____

Matthew 26:36-41 _____

Matthew 28:9-10 _____

Yes, a support group of friends can talk about anything. They can be real about themselves and real in sharing their need for prayer. What do the kinds of conversations Jesus had with his "support group" say to you about conversations between genuine friends?

On the lines below, write the names of people who are or could be part of your support system. (Don't look for "perfect" people.) You could get a luncheon group going as my friends did, or you could "collect" friends — individuals you have come to know whom you support in times of need and who will support you. (Remember, however, that there could be danger in making close friends with the opposite sex if either of you are married.) If possible, select several people so that you don't drain the energy of one or two. Also, it's important to have more than one friend because often when you have only one friend, she or he may be tempted to try to control you or you might be tempted to try to control that one friend.

Good Friend List

_____   _____   _____

_____   _____   _____

_____   _____   _____

Is there a crisis in your life right now? _____

Would it help to have someone to share it with? _____

Would you consider calling someone on the phone and asking him or her to pray for you? _____

If you're married, would you consider asking your spouse to pray with you? _____

Praying with another person may be the most humbling thing you've ever done. To get started, write out your opening words. "Hello, _____. This is _____. Do you have time to talk with me? I'm feeling (angry, hurt, fearful, etc.) _____. Will you _____ for me?"

Don't keep your friend on the phone more than seven minutes. This is for the sake of your further friendship. You don't want to exhaust her or him. Then look over your list of friends to see who you can call next time. If you've asked your spouse to pray with you, don't interrupt or contradict or add to her or his prayer. Thank your spouse with words and a hug.

How does this whole idea of asking for prayer make you feel?

_____

_____

_____

_____

_____

_____

In addition to prayer, we also need the help of others. The following is a good story about a famous person who was overextended and how help came to him.

Read Exodus 18:13-27. Let's reconstruct this story in contemporary language and try to read between the lines.

Jethro, Moses' father-in-law, decides to watch Moses in action one day. Jethro, in essence, asks, "What on earth are you doing?" in verse 14. He adds, "Why do you _____ _____?" Moses gives a familiar answer in verses 15 and 16: "The people _____, and I have to be there for them all. I mean I'm the only one who can do this."

Jethro replies in verse 17, "This is _____. You'll _____.

The work is too _____. You can't handle it alone. Listen to me. I've got an idea....Teach people to _____ you and that will make your _____ lighter because they will _____ it with you. You will be able to _____ and the people will be satisfied."

Moses listened to Jethro and: _____. After that Moses had enough time to take care of his wife and spend quality time with his sons. _____ went on his way alone.

Now, let's apply this story to your life. List here the names of any people who are becoming or already are a burden to you. After each person's name, write down *why* he or she is a burden.

1. _____. Because of _____

_____

_____

2. _____. Because of _____

_____

_____

3. _____. Because of _____

_____

_____

4. _____. Because of _____

_____

_____

Now here is my advice: Teach people to help you and that will ease your burden.

Plotting Out Your Plan for Getting Help

Before you can figure out who can help you, you need to ask four important questions about your work.

1. What am I doing that can only be done by me?

_____

_____

_____

_____

2. What am I doing that can be done by someone else?

_____

_____

_____

_____

_____

3. What am I doing that can be postponed?

_____

_____

_____

_____

4. What am I doing that no one needs to do at all?

_____

_____

_____

_____

_____

Now review what you wrote in number 2. List below the names of some people who could help you. If you have a spouse, she or he will often help, if asked. At work, if there's someone you can delegate work to, do it. If you have children who are old enough to do it, they can cook, shop, wash windows and floors, and run errands. What's more, it is good for them. Older people with time on their hands like to help and feel needed, even if they complain. Newcomers are eager to help out. Neighbors are often willing to work out an exchange arrangement as Virginia and I did. If you can afford it, consider hiring some help.

Here are the names of people who can help:

_____   _____

_____   _____

_____   _____

Make a note of whom you will train to help you (particularly children). Also, write here what kind of work you can trade or bargain for with someone else.

_____

_____

_____

_____

Wrap Up

Gaining control: On page 140 fill in the *I-Gain-Control-of-My-Life Chart* for lesson nine.

Continue during the week: Ask for at least one bit of help that will ease your burden. Also, pick up the phone and call someone to share a need and ask for prayer.

Just for fun: Ask someone you really like to go to lunch with you at a restaurant you've always wanted to experience.

Journal experience: Write about a past disappointment you had in a friendship. Rewrite that disappointment, giving it the best possible outcome.

Memorize:

If the one falls, the other will lift up his companion. Woe to the solitary man! For if he should fall, he has no one to lift him up.

(Ecclesiastes 4:10)

Closing prayer:

Dear God, help me shed my needlessly heavy burdens. Help me put into practice the ways that will lighten my load.

Glory be to the Father, and to the Son, and to the Holy Spirit, as it was in the beginning, is now, and ever shall be, world without end. Amen.

Lesson Ten
Making Peace
Through Reconciliation

Beginning prayer:

Dear God, please give me the strength and help I need to make peace in my world.

Glory be to the Father, and to the Son, and to the Holy Spirit, as it was in the beginning, is now, and ever shall be, world without end. Amen.

The Lesson: Asking for God's
Forgiveness Reduces Stress

My husband, Bill, looked out the window one morning and announced, "Uh-oh...the neighbor's dogs ripped open the plastic garbage bag I put out for the garbage collectors last night. Now there's garbage all over the yard."

In a cross voice I responded, "Well, why did you put the plastic sack out last night? You know the dogs always get into it. Why didn't you just wait and put it out this morning?"

After we came in from cleaning up egg shells and grimy orange peels, I apologized: "Bill, I was wrong to speak that way. I'm sorry for my sarcasm." But later when the house was quiet, I sensed the Lord saying, "Apology is not enough. You need to confess your sins and repent."

I told God I was truly sorry and that I wanted to turn away from hurting people with my words, especially my husband. With honesty and repentance, gone was an opportunity for the Enemy to tell me how horrible I am. Gone was the temptation to tell myself I'd failed again. Gone was the disquieting feeling of something between God and me being out of order. Honesty and repentance had kept me from feeling a great deal of needless stress.

But what does it mean to "repent"?

Read Luke 15:11-32. This is the famous parable of The Prodigal Son. One of the most important sentences in the story is found in verse 18. Reread it. What does the wayward son finally do in the story?

_____

_____

What can we assume the son did about his past life?

_____

_____

This is the real meaning of repentance — to return to God and leave behind a past way of life. If the son had come home with the express purpose of getting enough money to go back to the old life, he might have been sorry for his past but not repentant.

Sorrow for sin is good; to feel saddened at what we've done is definitely important. But sorrow is not enough to keep us from sinning again. We need to honestly name our wrongdoing so we can turn our backs on what we've done and promise, with the help of God's grace, not to go that way again. Then we have repented.

Read John 8:1-11. What were Jesus' final words to this woman?

_____

_____

Imagine that you are that woman, and after this encounter with Jesus, you return to your home. You have only this one way of making a living. What will you do now? Remember, your friends are going to encourage you to keep on as you've been doing. Write here your little story of what this woman does next. Read your story to a friend sometime during the next week.

_____

_____

_____

_____

_____

_____

Read Galatians 5:19-21. List here the sins mentioned in this passage.

_____

_____

_____

_____

_____

_____

Read Galatians 5:22-23. Write here what the fruits of the Spirit are.

_____

_____

_____

_____

_____

Now, spend some time in prayer. With the Holy Spirit's help, pick one sin from the long list you wrote on the previous page that describes the sin you most frequently commit. How would your stress level be different if this sin were out of your life?

_____

_____

_____

_____

_____

What is the opposite quality of this sin? Write out what difference it would make to your stress level if this quality were at work in your life.

_____

_____

_____

_____

_____

We can all work to increase virtues in our lives as we work to free ourselves from sin. Picture yourself walking up the staircase from sin to freedom. Look up each Scripture passage and write on the stairstep what it basically says.

            (5) Psalm 51:11 _____

          (4) 1 John 1:9 _____

       (3) 2 Corinthians 7:11 _____

    (2) Acts 26:20 _____

(1) Acts 3:19 _____

Now, try to sequentially apply what each Scripture passage said to an incident in your own life. As an example, let's take my sin toward Bill mentioned in the beginning of this chapter.

(1) God, I confess my sin of angry words toward my husband.
(2) I want to return to your ways and do something to atone for what I've done. (I decided to write Bill a little note of love and tuck it in his lunch.)
(3) Thank you for totally forgiving me and cleansing me from this sin.
(4) Lord, I admit I was wrong. I know you can forgive and cleanse me.
(5) I praise you, Lord, for returning a guilt-free heart to me.

Now try it out for yourself. Find a quiet place and prayerfully bring to the Lord the sin you wrote about on page 117. Write what you conclude from Scripture passages 1-5 on page 119.

(1) _____

(2) _____

(3) _____

(4) _____

(5) _____

Wrap Up

Gaining control: On page 140 fill in the *I-Gain-Control-of-My-Life Chart* for lesson ten.

Continue during the week: This is important. Take the message of this lesson to the sacrament of penance/reconciliation. This will help you heal and give you the grace to repent and change. Make sure you carry through with truly *repenting*. That means you genuinely turn (or do your best to turn) away from doing the same thing again. If you find you have "blown it" and committed the same sin once more, then go through the Scripture steps again. Note how much longer it takes you before you commit that same sin again (five minutes to three weeks or longer). After each session of honesty and repentance — of really wanting to turn your back on that sin — the length of time before committing it again will grow larger.

Just for fun: Buy or pick yourself a flower, or take a half day off from work and go have fun at the zoo.

Journal experience: Tell Christ how much you enjoy being reconciled with him. Record his response to you.

Memorize:

Rend your hearts, not your garments,
and return to the LORD, your God.
For gracious and merciful is he,
slow to anger, rich in kindness,
and relenting in punishment.

(Joel 2:13)

Closing prayer:

Dear God, thank you for this lesson. It was good to face you and myself.

Glory be to the Father, and to the Son, and to the Holy Spirit, as it was in the beginning, is now, and ever shall be, world without end. Amen.

Lesson Eleven
Letting Go of the Past Through Forgiveness

Beginning prayer:

Dear God, forgive us our debts as we forgive our debtors.

Glory be to the Father, and to the Son, and to the Holy Spirit, as it was in the beginning, is now, and ever shall be, world without end. Amen.

The Lesson:
Clinging to Past Hurts Causes Stress

A man I'll call Vince was deeply wounded by a violent outburst from his teenage son, Andy. Vince is a sincere Christian and, as crushed as he was by the hatred on Andy's face and the terrible words the boy had hurled at him, Vince went to God right away, praying, "Father, I forgive him. I put him in your hands. I ask you to heal his life."

Vince told his wife, his daughter, and me how much he trusted God and how totally he had forgiven Andy. Three days after the incident, Vince woke up with a feeling of something being wrong with his back and legs. They ached, and all Vince felt like doing was sitting in front of the television with a heating pad behind his back.

Finally, Vince knew something was really bothering him when one Saturday morning he blew up at his wife for leaving the lid off the peanut butter jar. He thought, *I'll eat breakfast and read the paper. Then I'll feel better.* But what had helped him relax in the past didn't help this time. He still felt physically upset. Next, Vince even picked up a Bible and tried to pray, but the feeling of something being wrong inside of himself persisted.

Vince decided to go down to the YMCA and sit in the whirlpool. Lying back in the hot relaxing water, he prayed, thinking, *Lord, what is it?* He received a strong impression that he was still angry with Andy and that he needed to forgive his son. *But I've already done that,* he argued. *If I've already forgiven him, how can I be angry?* But the impression to forgive grew stronger until Vince knew he had to comply. *Lord...*he silently prayed as the hot water churned around him, *I forgive my son again for those angry words. I don't hold them against him.* He paused, then prayed, *Now, Jesus, I want to again trust him to your care.* With that prayer came the peace that had eluded Vince for days.

What had happened was this. When we're hurt either physically or emotionally, our bodies go into shock. That's their protection from feeling the pain. (A baby zebra chased by a lion goes into such shock that by the time the lion reaches it, the baby zebra doesn't feel the pain of the kill.)

After shock comes denial. It's part of our protective system too. It's like a built-in super-strength aspirin for our emotions. When we take painkillers for our headaches, the pain doesn't actually go away. Instead, the medicine only blocks the pain so that we can't feel it. Denial does the same thing. It is a subconscious reaction that says, "I don't care what the facts are. This whole thing is not that bad" or "I know others may be upset by this, but it's no big deal to me."

If we say we forgive while we're still in shock or still denying what's happened, then we will still have anger toward the person who has hurt us, even if we say we've forgiven them.

The first time Vince forgave his son, and that was the right thing to do, he was only able to forgive Andy to the point of the pain he was then feeling. But when the shock and denial were not present to block the pain, then Vince finally began feeling all the stress symptoms that shock and denial had covered up. That's why he needed to "return to the scene of the crime" — go back to the stressful time — and forgive again. Once that was done, he felt free.

But what might happen next? If Andy returned and was again churlish and unrepentant, or if he returned and acted as though nothing were wrong, Vince would likely deal with his response subconsciously. Once more his body would feel it. (Heart, liver, pancreas, endocrine system, digestion, muscles — all become involved.) In addition to doing all the things this book talks about to help our bodies in stress, Vince will need to forgive again.

If he and his son can come together in agreement, asking each other's forgiveness (in words or actions), then the whole thing can be settled to the relief of Vince's body. But as long as this situation endures, Vince will need to consciously forgive every time he realizes he hurts. The physical penalty for not forgiving is obvious. The spiritual reward for this kind of continuing forgiveness must be enormous.

No matter how often we pray, no matter what we entrust to God's keeping, no matter what and who we forgive…it should not be a surprise to us that when we get through shock and past denial, we will have to pray. We will have to hand things over to God and forgive again.

Note: If a dangerous pattern of abuse such as alcoholism, beating and battering, drug addiction, or sexual abuse has begun, then the wounded person needs to seek outside help for herself or himself. Forgiveness does *not* mean that you have to endure someone else's dangerously abusive behavior. It is *not* "weak" to admit that you need help. In fact, going for help is a deeply responsible action. If you are in an abusive situation, I recommend that you read the book *Codependent No More: How to Stop Controlling Others and Start Caring for Yourself* by Melody

Beattie. For outside help in dealing with someone who drinks too much, contact Al-Anon, a support group for people affected by someone else's drinking; Alateen, for teenagers affected by someone's drinking; Al-Atots, for children affected by someone's drinking (this group exists in only a few areas). There are also Overeaters Anonymous, for people affected by eating disorders; Families Anonymous, for people concerned about the use of chemicals and/or related behavioral problems in a relative or friend; Adult Children of Alcoholics, for adult children of alcoholics; Co-SA, for people affected by another person's sexual addiction; Gam-Anon, for people affected by another person's gambling; Parents Anonymous, for parents who are abusive, neglectful or afraid of becoming so, or for adolescents who are encountering problems due to past or current abuse. If you decide to attend any of these groups' meetings, attend the meetings six times before you decide whether it's for you. That's because first impressions can be misleading. Yet if you don't feel the "chemistry" is right after six meetings, feel free to try a different group that meets for the same purpose.

Read Matthew 18:21-22. In this passage, Jesus has some advice for Peter on how often we are to forgive each person who hurts us. What do you think Jesus is really saying here?

_____ Forgive each person seven times seventy.

_____ Forgive each person seventy-seven times.

_____ Forgive as often as it takes to fully forgive.

In the story about Vince and Andy, how many more times do you think Vince will have to forgive his son? _____

What do you think will happen to Vince's body if he decides that any more forgiveness is just too hard to do?

_____

_____

If Vince does continue to forgive his son, what kind of spiritual reward do you think he'll receive? (*Hint:* Read 1 John 3:24 and James 1:25.)

_____

_____

_____

Now let's read another interesting story about forgiveness.

Read Genesis 27:1-35. What did Jacob steal?

_____

Read Genesis 27:41. What was Esau's response?

_____

_____

Read Genesis 33:1-4. Many years have gone by and Jacob is still afraid of Esau's retribution. How does Esau greet him?

_____

_____

Is it ever too late to forgive someone? _____

Read Luke 23:34. What did Jesus ask for the men who tortured him?

_____

Is there anything that is just too terrible for you to forgive?

_____

Read Matthew 18:23-35. How does God look at a person who won't forgive others? _____

Are you finding it impossible to forgive anyone in your life? ____

If so, who is it and why is it so hard to forgive this person?____

_____

Read Acts 7:56-60—8:1. Who gave approval for the stoning of Stephen? _____

What were Stephen's last words before he died?

_____

_____

Saul, once he converted to Christianity, changed his name to Paul. Some say that Stephen's forgiveness of Saul opened the door for Paul's wide ministry. What are your thoughts on this?

_____

_____

_____

_____

On the spaces below, write out the effects that your forgiveness could possibly have on the outcome of the lives of the persons you forgive.

Name	Hurt	Possible effect of forgiveness in that person's life.	Possible effect that forgiveness of another will have in your life.
_____	_____	_____	_____
_____	_____	_____	_____
_____	_____	_____	_____
_____	_____	_____	_____

Read Ephesians 4:32. When we forgive, how should that forgiveness be done?

_____

_____

Will you now forgive each person on your list from your heart and with compassion?

_____

Remember, it takes energy to hold a grudge or to hate. What can you expect to happen *in your body* when you forgive?

_____

What could be the physical consequences of refusing to get rid of grudges or hatred?

_____

Wrap Up

Gaining control: On page 140 fill in the *I-Gain-Control-of-My-Life Chart* for lesson eleven.

Continue during the week: People needing your forgiveness will continue to come to your mind. Write these down in this workbook, and as you forgive each person, draw a line through his or her name.

Just for fun: For a change, get out the Monopoly game or some other board game and get the family or a group of friends involved.

Journal experience: Give yourself seventy-two hours to really notice the difference once you've forgiven someone. Then record in your journal how you feel *physically* now that the worst is forgiven. Note how well you sleep, how your appetite improves, how your body pain eases, how your sense of well-being improves, how your joyful times increase, and anything else that's significant.

Memorize:
> Be kind to one another, compassionate, forgiving one another as God has forgiven you in Christ.
>
> (Ephesians 4:32)

Closing prayer:
Dear God, I ask you to bless in a special way those persons I've forgiven. Thank you for this all-important opportunity.

Glory be to the Father, and to the Son, and to the Holy Spirit, as it was in the beginning, is now, and ever shall be, world without end. Amen.

Lesson Twelve
The Secret of Energy

Beginning prayer:
Dear God, thank you for loving me just the way I am.

Glory be to the Father, and to the Son, and to the Holy Spirit, as it was in the beginning, is now, and ever shall be, world without end. Amen.

The Lesson: Putting Balance and
Trust in Your Life

Our Lenten study group decided that for Easter we would blitz an indigent family with help. There was a disabled father, a young mother, and four boys. Each person in the study group took responsibility for one part of the blitz — Easter dinner, household needs, Easter baskets, toys, and clothing. My area of concern was household needs. The day I had set aside to visit, I was weary and not looking forward to it. The family, however, welcomed me warmly. The first obvious need was a window covering. That was easy; my mother's basement held a box of drapes that only needed to be pressed. The family was so excited about drapes at the window that I couldn't help being excited too. I took one of the boys to buy the drapery rod, and while we were at the store I asked him about towels: "Do you need any?"

"Well, we have two, I think," the boy responded.

"What's your mother's favorite color?"

"Pink."

What a joy it was to bring that family six new pink towels, washcloths, dishtowels, and a potholder with little hearts on it. The mother couldn't believe her eyes. She held the towels close, but it was the potholder that brought tears. Next, she and I scrounged about the Goodwill store and other places for a chest of drawers, a lamp, and a little table. I picked up some light bulbs; there were no working light bulbs in the house, not even in the windowless bathroom. I found that getting this household normalized was fun. Being with these people energized me. There was strength and joy in the work.

This probably seems like a strange story to tell after all the lessons on saying no, getting priorities straight, and using energy wisely. What I want to say here is that *everyone* has a gift or talent to use on behalf of others. *One* project that uses that gift (*not* two or three or four projects) is good for all of us. Let's look at a story we know well.

Read Matthew 25:14-30. Where do the talents we are entrusted with come from?

_____

What are we to do with the talents (gifts) God gives us?

_____

_____

What happens to the gift that is not used?

_____

Who, then, gets it? _____

Our talents must first be used in our immediate family. That is where talents develop. The parable of The Talents shows us that when we develop personal talents, we receive more. As those talents develop and multiply, the Lord will, from time to time, give us a special way to use them.

Assess your talents and write them down here. (My talent in this lesson's opening story was knowing how to shop for bargains.)

_____

_____

_____

_____

Using Your Talents: A Balancing Act

There is an important balance that each one of us has to find. It's like balancing on a teetertotter. On the one hand, if we don't use our gifts, we never build up enough joy to get off the ground. On the other hand, if we overburden ourselves by using our talents until we're exhausted, we'll get so weary that the work will override the joy.

Below is a drawing of a teetertotter. On it, write out what special way you could use your talents that would balance with the joy that using them would bring.

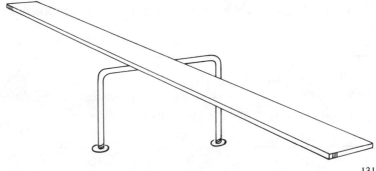

Now, write out the steps that *you* could take that might make you get overburdened and thereby diminish the joy you'd find in using your talents. (Everyone's steps to being overburdened are different, so don't feel like there's only one right answer to this.)

_____

_____

_____

_____

The balance between doing what brings us joy and overdoing it is extremely delicate. It requires regular fine-tuning. Trial and error are the best teachers. Don't feel bad if you miss the balance and get carried away. Just say no to the overcommitment, give your body rest and care, and try again. With practice and prayer you will find the right balance to bring you the joy that restores your energy.

Making Sure Christ Is Part of the Process

Read Matthew 14:3-13. In this passage, Jesus hears the stressful news of John the Baptist's beheading. What is the first thing Jesus does?

_____

Read Matthew 14:14-23. What does Jesus do after the whole incredible day of teaching more than five thousand people and then feeding them?

_____

Read Mark 1:32-35. After an extremely exhausting schedule the day before, Jesus awakens before dawn and does what?

_____

Was anyone with him? _____

How did Jesus get strength from prayer when praying takes energy?

_____

_____

How do we pray and find our strength renewed? (See Matthew 11:28-30 for some hints.)

_____

_____

_____

Read Isaiah 40:31. What is going to happen to those who wait on or maintain hope in the Lord?

_____

_____

_____

Sharing the Burden With Jesus

Jesus said that he would give us rest if we bring him the burdens and crises that sap our energy. On page 143 is a cross that belongs to you and Jesus. On that cross you can place all your needs.

On the horizontal beam (where Jesus' hands were nailed), write out the names of the people who have hurt you and whom you need to forgive for the first or the fiftieth time.

On the vertical beam (where Jesus' body lay), write out what is causing you too much stress. Difficult transitions, nonreciprocity, ambiguity, sickness, suffering...anything that stresses you should be written here.

In the circle at the center of the cross (where the heart of Jesus lay), write down your own sins for which you still need to ask forgiveness.

At the top of the cross (where Jesus' head lay), write down any beneath-the-surface sorrows like failures, disappointments, and regrets — those times that you wish with all your heart you could go back and do differently.

Now put your hands on that cross that you now share with Jesus. It's time to pray:

Dear Jesus, here are my burdens. I bring them to you. I ask you to forgive my sins. I ask you to heal my life. I ask for the rest you have promised me.

Now just rest quietly to wait and listen before the Lord for a few minutes. The Lord speaks to people in many ways.

- To some he assures forgiveness.
- To some he speaks words of direction.
- He asks some to truly forgive again.

But to all, Jesus gives words of encouragement and strength. Respond to him, telling him what is in your heart. Listen to further words and continue to rest until you feel new strength. In your journal write down whatever message you believe Jesus wants you to understand. You can bring him your burdens and wait upon him every day of your life. In time you will run and not be weary. In time you will be able to handle the stresses of your life.

Wrap Up

Gaining control: On page 140 fill in the *I-Gain-Control-of-My-Life Chart* for lesson twelve. Tear the chart out and keep it someplace handy like the back of the bedroom door. That way you can refer to it often.

Continue on: Here are some comforting Scripture passages you can use in your prayer time, to help you through stressful situations, or to use in any way you find helpful. You can also use them as short affirmative prayers, reciting them slowly and thoughtfully.

- God is our refuge and our strength,
    an ever-present help in distress (Psalm 46:2).

- Fear not, I am with you;
    be not dismayed; I am your God.
  I will strengthen you, and help you,
    and uphold you with my right hand of justice (Isaiah 41:10).

- We know that all things work for good for those who love God,
  who are called according to his purpose (Romans 8:28).

- For I am convinced that neither death, nor life, nor angels, nor
  principalities, nor present things, nor future things, nor powers,
  nor height, nor depth, nor any other creature will be able
  to separate us from the love of God in Christ Jesus our Lord
  (Romans 8:38-39).

- The LORD is my shepherd; I shall not want.
    In verdant pastures he gives me repose;
  Beside restful waters he leads me;
    he refreshes my soul.
  He guides me in right paths
    for his name's sake.
  Even though I walk in the dark valley
    I fear no evil; for you are at my side
  With your rod and your staff
    that give me courage.
  You spread the table before me
    in the sight of my foes;
  You anoint my head with oil;
    my cup overflows.

Only goodness and kindness follow me
  all the days of my life;
And I shall dwell in the house of the LORD
  for years to come (Psalm 23).

Just for fun: Find a sunset or the view from the attic or from the top of a hill or from a beach or some other nice vantage point. Soak up the beauty of God's handiwork.

Journal experience: Write out one of the Scripture passages from pages 135 and 136. Then wait upon the Lord for what he wants to say, especially to you, about that Scripture. Write out what you believe God is telling you, then respond to it in writing.

Memorize:
  They that hope in the LORD will renew their strength,
    they will soar as with eagles' wings;
  They will run and not grow weary,
    walk and not grow faint (Isaiah 40:31).

Closing prayer:
  Dear God, thank you for these twelve weeks, for what I've learned and for the changes in my life.
  Glory be to the Father, and to the Son, and to the Holy Spirit, as it was in the beginning, is now, and ever shall be, world without end. Amen.

Continuing On:
Helps for Further Progress

Even though this workbook is ending, your struggles to regain energy will continue because *it takes a long, long time to get your strength back after you have been exhausted by the struggles and cares of life.*

It's as if you are just a little chicken with little chicken legs, and you have set your mind to walk from the East Coast to the West Coast. Family and friends may cheer you on saying, "You can do that easily in six months." But you are starting out just a little chicken with little chicken legs. If at the end of six months you've only passed through a few towns, your friends may get disappointed. They may think you should be moving faster. If this happens, remember that *you are moving at your own speed.* Nobody else's opinions matter. You will make it in God's time as you take care of your body, rest, say no, forgive your enemies, seek God's forgiveness, and wait upon the Lord.

Here are some nourishing Scripture tidbits for you to eat along the way as you need them. Just take one at a time.

To be assured of the Lord's presence:
- Deuteronomy 31:6
- Psalm 9:9-10
- Isaiah 43:2

- Matthew 28:20
- John 14:18-21
- Hebrews 13:5

To be assured of the Lord's love:
- Zephaniah 3:17
- John 14:21
- 1 Corinthians 2:9
- 1 John 4:10

To be assured of the Lord's care:
- Psalm 55:23
- Romans 8:16-17
- Philippians 1:6
- 1 Thessalonians 5:16-18

To be assured of the Lord's help:
- Isaiah 41:8-14
- John 14:27
- Romans 15:13
- Ephesians 2:13-14
- Philippians 4:6-7

To be assured of the Lord's guidance:
- Psalm 32:8
- Proverbs 16:3
- Ecclesiastes 2:26
- Isaiah 30:20
- Isaiah 42:16

Further Reading

Beattie, Melody. *Codependent No More: How to Stop Controlling Others and Start Caring for Yourself.* New York: Harper and Row, 1988.

Hansel, Tim. *When I Relax I Feel Guilty.* Elgin, Ill.: David C. Cook Publishing Company, 1979.

Hart, Archibald. *Adrenalin and Stress.* Irving, Tex.: Word Books, 1986.

King, Pat. *Help for Women With Too Much to Do.* Liguori, Mo.: Liguori Publications, 1988.

Leman, Kevin. *Bonkers.* New York: Dell Publishing Company, 1989.

McQuade, Walter and Ann Aikman. *Stress.* New York: Bantam Books, 1975.

Minirth, Frank, and others. *How to Beat Burnout.* Chicago: Moody Press, 1986.

Ogilvie, Lloyd J. *Making Stress Work for You: Ten Proven Principles.* Irving, Tex.: Word Books, 1984.

Ornish, Dean. *Stress, Diet and Your Heart.* New York: Signet Books (New American Library), 1984.

Sehnert, Keith W. *Stress-Unstress.* Minneapolis: Augsburg Fortress Publishing House, 1981.

The I-Gain-Control-of-My-Life Chart

This is the
way my body responds
to stress.

Lesson One _____

_____

_____

_____

These are
the stresses of
my life.

Lesson Two _____

_____

_____

Lesson Three _____

_____

_____

_____

Lesson Four _____

_____

_____

_____

These are my
helpful responses
to the stresses
my body is under.

Lesson Five _____

_____

_____

_____

Lesson Six _____

_____

_____

_____

Lesson Seven _____

_____

_____

_____

Lesson Eight _____

_____

_____

_____

Lesson Nine _____

_____

_____

_____

This is how I cooperate with God so that I can be healed.

Lesson Ten _____

_____

_____

_____

Lesson Eleven _____

_____

_____

_____

Lesson Twelve _____

_____

_____

_____

My Scripture verse for times of stress is:

_____

_____

_____

_____

Sharing the Burden With Jesus

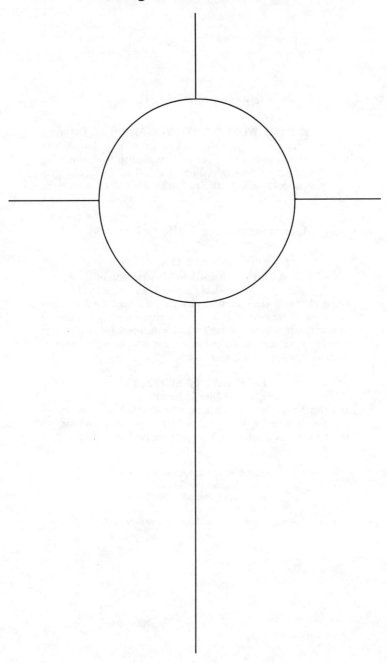

By the same author...

HELP FOR WOMEN WITH TOO MUCH TO DO

This book reveals how the author — a mother of ten — learned how to reduce stress and increase personal satisfaction by restructuring her life and her attitudes. She offers practical advice on changing lifestyle, outlook, and expectations to meet life with renewed vigor. **$3.95**

More resources for dealing with stress...

INNER CALM
A Christian Answer to Modern Stress
by Dr. Paul DeBlassie, III

Using clear terms and practical examples, this book discusses how stress can often cause the most common physical and psychological problems experienced in today's world. It then explains, step by step, how to reduce stress and experience inner calm through the use of the time-honored Jesus Prayer. **$4.95**

PATHWAYS TO SERENITY
by Philip St. Romain

Drawing from Christian, Eastern, psychological, and ethical approaches to serenity, this book outlines a practical road map to finding peace of mind through the peace of the Lord. **$4.95**

Order from your local bookstore or write to:
Liguori Publications
Box 060, Liguori, MO 63057-9999
*(Please add $1.00 for postage and handling for
orders under $5.00; $1.50 for orders over $5.00.)*